Mary Agatha Pennell

Maud Hamilton, or Self-will and its consequences

Mary Agatha Pennell

Maud Hamilton, or Self-will and its consequences

ISBN/EAN: 9783741191848

Manufactured in Europe, USA, Canada, Australia, Japa

Cover: Foto ©Andreas Hilbeck / pixelio.de

Manufactured and distributed by brebook publishing software (www.brebook.com)

Mary Agatha Pennell

Maud Hamilton, or Self-will and its consequences

Maud Hamilton;

or,

Self-Will

AND ITS CONSEQUENCES.

BY

MARY AGATHA PENNELL,

AUTHOR OF "ELSIE McDERMOTT;" "BERTRAM ELDON;"
"AGNES WILMOTT;" &c.

———:o:———

London:
THOMAS RICHARDSON AND SON,
23, King Edward Street, City, E.C.;
AND DERBY.

To my Nieces,

EVELINE AND MABEL,

This Tale is Affectionately Dedicated

BY THE AUTHOR.

CONTENTS.

CHAPTER I.
A Chapter of Accidents 1

CHAPTER II.
First Impressions of Riversdale; or, "Lessons! Lessons! from Morning till Night" 14

CHAPTER III.
Up to Mischief again 27

CHAPTER IV.
Maud's Birthday.—The Picnic at Seaforth 41

CHAPTER V.
Important Events.—Ben Ward's Refusal ... 60

CHAPTER VI.
Self-Will and its Consequences 77

CHAPTER VII.
In the Storm; or, Life and Death ... 92

CHAPTER VIII.
Off to School 115

Maud Hamilton;

OR,
SELF-WILL AND ITS CONSEQUENCES.

———:o:———

CHAPTER I.

A Chapter of Accidents.

Maud Hamilton was comfortably seated on the hearth-rug, in front of a nice bright fire, one hand resting on the shaggy-haired dog, her pet and play-fellow, which lay curled up by her side, enjoying the warmth as much as his little mistress. Maud was much interested in a story-book which her cousin Hilda had lent her, and congratulated herself on having a quiet hour in which she would enjoy reading the adventures of "The Runaway." In a short time, however, she was interrupted by her sister Edith coming into the room, and exclaiming, "Oh, Maud! do come and help me, or the packing will never be finished."

But Maud, instead of getting up, only raised

her eyes off the book for a minute, saying, "You *must* manage without me for the present. I am so dreadfully interested, I cannot possibly leave off in the middle of this chapter. The 'Runaway' has just made her escape, and I must read on until I see how it will all end."

Having said this Maud settled herself again, and was soon wrapped up in Olga's history.

Edith, knowing it was useless to say anything more, returned to her work alone. She felt somewhat disheartened as she re-entered the large play-room, which up to the present time had been the children's usual resort when their daily lessons were ended.

"How tiresome," she said to herself, "that Maud will read that stupid book when she ought to be busy. I suppose I had better begin without her." And Edith commenced taking down from the shelves of a cupboard a number of toys and books. It was hard and tedious work, and very dirty and dusty she made herself. Having partly filled a box, she sat down to rest, when presently Maud came running in.

"Edith," she exclaimed, "do not trouble yourself to pack up many of *my* things, for I have quite made up my mind to follow Olga's example, and run away from school. I am *so* glad I have read the book, for now I know exactly how to manage everything, and shall

A CHAPTER OF ACCIDENTS. 3

begin this very day to practice how to let myself down from the bedroom window."

Edith looked rather grave, for she knew too well how fond her sister was of getting into mischief.

"I mean what I say," continued Maud, "and it's no use your sitting there looking like a judge. I tell you what, Miss Edith; I expect when you find yourself at school, with no end of lessons to get through, you will only be too thankful to make your escape, and join me. Come, leave the rest of the work till to-morrow, and follow me. If you will only do *exactly* as I tell you, we shall manage beautifully."

Maud then shut up the box, and, accompanied by her sister, led the way until they reached a bedroom which was at the further end of the passage. Carefully locking the door to prevent any interruption, Maud began dragging the clothes off the bed.

"Maud! what are you going to do?" asked her sister.

"Patience, my dear, and you will soon see. These two sheets,"—and Maud held them up,— "must be strongly tied together, one end fastened to the bed-post, the other round my waist, and you just watch me whilst I let myself down from the window."

"Oh pray, Maud, don't do anything so dangerous," pleaded Edith. "If you were to fall you might hurt yourself dreadfully. Remember, you promised mamma before she left that you would be steady, and not worry nurse. Only a week has passed, and you are already breaking your word."

But all Edith said was in vain. Maud declared that if she had read the story of the "Runaway" before her mamma had gone to India she never would have promised not to have done this.

"Well, then," said Edith, "I shall *not* remain with you, but go downstairs." And to Maud's dismay, she opened the door, leaving her sister alone.

"How ill-natured of Edith," muttered Maud. "But never mind, I'll practice without her. If *she* is afraid of falling, *I* am not. Olga had terrible trials to go through, and I mean to be like her, and not a coward. I must make haste, though, or nurse will be coming up and stopping me. As I have no one to help me with the sheets, I must try and climb down, holding on to the ivy; I believe it's very strong, and will do just as well."

Maud now opened the window, and whilst she is making the attempt to let herself down into the garden, we will leave her for a few minutes.

A CHAPTER OF ACCIDENTS.

It did not take Edith long to find Nurse Grey, who was busily engaged in her own room.

"Well, my dear," she asked, as Edith entered, "whatever makes you look so white? Is anything the matter?"

"I am afraid something *will* be the matter if you don't go to Maud at once," replied the little girl. And then, having related what had happened, nurse hurried with Edith to the room in which Maud had locked herself up.

Many times Nurse Grey knocked at the door, desiring Maud to open it, but not receiving any answer, she said, "I think, my dear, we'd best go down into the garden and look for her there, for certain sure she ain't in the room."

On reaching the garden, they saw Maud in the distance, lying on the path just underneath the window from which she had been attempting to descend. Nurse Grey's hands went up in despair when she saw the plight that young lady was in. Maud's frock was torn from top to bottom, besides being covered with dirt and gravel.

"Don't be frightened, nurse," she called out; "there's not much the matter."

"Bless my heart," said the old woman, "did I ever see the like o' this? Miss Maud, you wears me out entirely, *that* you do, with these wild ways of yours. No one would believe you'd been brought up in a Christian country. Here you be, a perfect sight of dirt and rags. It's a mighty wonder you ain't broke your neck: but I believe before you've done you'll come to some untimely end. And mark *me*, Miss Maud, as sure as I'm a standing on this yer gravel path, I'll write and tell your aunt Milicent."

"*Please*, nurse, don't be angry with me this time. If the ivy hadn't given way, I should have climbed down quite safely, without tearing my frock one bit. I'll try and mend it to-morrow, and promise you *faithfully* to be *quite* steady for a long time."

"No, no, missie; I ain't got a bit of faith in *none* of your promises. You only makes them one day, to be broken the next."

Maud, seeing nurse was not to be pacified, knew she had better be silent, and submit to the order she received to go to bed for the rest of the day. Very disconsolate the little girl felt when she went to her room to pass so many hours alone, for Edith was not allowed to go near her. The next morning Maud appeared at the breakfast table somewhat subdued, not knowing if she would still be considered in disgrace. When breakfast was finished, she asked nurse if she should begin mending her frock.

"Well, my dear, I *did* intend you should do

so; but it was in such a state of dirt that there was no getting a needle into it, and Susan has put it into water. The best thing you and Miss Edith can do is to go out into the garden; and all I beg you young ladies is to keep straight to-day, for I can't bear no more worry. I have a world of work to get through, so must go and be busy." And with this nurse left the room.

Maud was delighted at this arrangement, and settled with Edith they should take their hoops and go out at once. For some time the children amused themselves by running races, but after a while Maud declared she was tired of doing the same sort of thing over and over again. "I know what I shall do," she said; "just go and ask John to let me have 'Prince.' I should so much enjoy a gallop round the meadow."

"I don't think," replied Edith, "you will get him to leave his work to saddle the pony this morning."

"Well, then, I can manage without the saddle, for a ride I *must* and *will* have," said Maud. And away she went in search of the gardener, whilst Edith returned to the house, to amuse herself with her needlework.

Very soon Maud caught sight of John, and making her way up to him, made her wishes known. But John refused, and was not to be coaxed into taking the pony out, although she said all she could think of to make the old man relent.

"No, no, missy; I ain't a going to do any such thing." And he dug away harder than ever.

"Well, then," said Maud, "will you let me just go into the stable and see 'Prince,' if I may not have him to ride on? Say yes this once. You know, John, very soon I am going away, and then you will be sorry you were so unkind." And Maud put her little hand on the gardener's.

It was not often the old man held out, but this time he was firm, for nurse had told him about Maud's behaviour the previous evening. "Look here, missie," he said, as he stopped digging for a minute or two, "if you was to go on a talking till midnight, nothing will make me go from my word. I've told you I won't allow no pony out to-day, and I means what I says; so now you'd much better go along in doors with Miss Edith, for if you bides in the garden you'll be up to some mischief, I feel certain of it."

Well would it have been for the little girl if she had done as she was told; but when once she set her heart on having anything, it was seldom she gave up her own will.

Maud walked slowly away towards the stables,

for she thought to herself, "If I can manage it I will get in and see my darling pony. I never thought John was such a horrid, cross old man. But, dear me, I do believe I see the key in the stable door. How capital! Yes, there it is! Now then, Mr. John, after all I shall have a ride."

Maud lost no time, fearing John might be coming to the stable; so, quickly unfastening the rope by which the pony was tied, sprang on his back, and the next minute "Prince," with his little mistress, was trotting across the yard and out into the meadow beyond. The wilful child congratulated herself on having gained her own way. She was enjoying a good canter round and round the field, when she was spied by John in the distance, who stood watching her in amazement.

"Well, I never!" said the old man; "if that child ain't beyond all I ever come across; there's no doing nothing with her. Depend upon it, I've been and forgot to take that 'ere key out of the door, and little miss has got her own way as usual. The only thing I can do is to go at once, and tell her, as firm like as I can, that she is to give up directly, and get off the pony."

Having come to this determination, John, bidding the stable boy, who was working close by, to follow him, so that he might take charge of the animal, whilst he himself saw Maud safely into the house, walked off to the meadow, where Miss Maud was now in high glee, galloping away to her heart's content, unheedful of all danger.

Before he could make her hear or see him, the pony was suddenly startled by the firing of a gun in an adjoining field, and dashed off at full speed. Maud held on as firmly as she could, and might have succeeded in keeping her seat, had not "Prince" stumbled, throwing her with great violence to the ground. John hastened to where Maud lay quite unconscious, saying, as he walked along, that he felt sure from the first that bad would come of Miss Maud's goings on. Sending the boy to tell nurse what had happened, he tried to lift the little girl in his arms; but every movement caused her to moan with pain, so he waited until nurse should arrive, when he hoped to be able to manage something whereby she could be carried home with greater ease.

Nurse Grey was not altogether surprised when she heard of the accident, for Edith had told her of Maud's determination to go for a ride. Having ascertained from the lad what had taken place, she at once accompanied him to the field, taking a small mattress on which to place the little sufferer.

Poor Maud lay moaning with pain; she had regained consciousness, and when nurse went up to her burst into tears. "Oh, nurse, *don't* be angry with me; I am punished already for being wilful with the dreadful pain I am in."

"Ah, my dear," replied the old woman, "I ain't a going to cast no reproaches on you in the midst of your sufferings; *they* will be a better sermon than I can preach; but it seems to me as if you gets worser and worser every day. Whatever would your ma say if she could see you as you are now? Come, John," she said to the gardener, "lift up the poor lamb as gently as you can on to the mattress, for the sooner she is home the better."

Very carefully was the little girl carried back to the house, and laid on her bed. The doctor who came to see Maud that evening, ascertained that she had sprained her foot; but beyond that and a few bruises there was nothing more serious to fear. It would be necessary for her to keep on the sofa for some time, and then in all probability she would be well again in the course of a few weeks. But lying on the sofa day after day was very irksome to the impatient child, and often tears trickled down her cheeks. Poor Maud felt more sad and down-hearted than I can put into words. Edith did all in her power to make it as little tedious as possible. Sometimes they would employ themselves with needlework, for they were making various presents to give to those from whom they would so soon be parted. Not only were their young friends to be remembered, but old John and his wife were also to come in for a gift. Nurse Grey insisted on Edith going every day for a walk, and it was during her sister's absence that Maud would bemoan her sad fate.

"Now, missie," said nurse one day, when on entering the room she found the little girl tossing about from side to side, "Why don't you lie down and be quiet? You'll worry yourself into a fever."

But there was no quietness for Maud. Although she opened the book handed to her by Nurse Grey, it was closed again in a few minutes, and at last she threw it from her, and buried her face in the cushion.

"Oh, dear me," she exclaimed, with a great weary sigh, "how dull and wretched it is here, nothing to see, nothing to hear, and nothing to do. I wish mamma had not gone to India, and settled to send us to Aunt Milicent's, and then all this would not have happened. Of course I wanted to have a ride on my pony, when I shall be leaving him so soon; and now I am laid up with this sprained foot." And with another

A CHAPTER OF ACCIDENTS. 13

fling Maud turned round, and threw her head once more on the pillow nurse had just arranged so nicely for her.

"If you would but keep still," said nurse, "there might be some chance of your getting better. You have no one but yourself to blame for the pain, so if I were you I would try and bear it patiently. If you had listened to what you were told, and given up your own way, all this trouble would not have happened."

"If John hadn't been so cross and ill-natured," cried Maud, indignantly, "I should not have had the fall." For it seemed to her but poor consolation that her sufferings might have been avoided if she had not been so self-willed. The pain was no better to bear for that, rather worse, if anything. "And," continued the little girl, "I am sure it's impossible to be patient when I have to lie here, with nothing to do, from morning till night."

"Yes, my dear," replied the kind old woman, as she kissed the excited child, and with a firm but gentle hand laid her back on the sofa, "it is *hard* to be so, but not *impossible*, when we remember who it is that has promised to help us. But I trust, please God, that very soon your foot will be better, and that you will have learned a lesson which will not soon be forgotten."

Maud listened whilst Nurse Grey was speaking to her, and then lay still, looking into the old woman's face.

"Nursie," she said, "I *will* try and bear patiently all I have to suffer, for I know I deserve to be punished for being so naughty." And the little girl, in her eagerness to assure nurse of the good resolutions she was making, raised herself into a sitting posture, and threw her arms round her nurse's neck.

I am glad to say Maud kept the promise made that day, and was never heard to murmur or complain during the rest of the time she had to keep quiet.

CHAPTER II.

First Impressions of Ribersdale; or, "Lessons, Lessons, from Morning till Night."

At the end of a month Maud's foot was quite well; she was able to run about again as usual; and it was decided they should leave B—— in a few days. Edith and Maud set to work immediately, tying up in parcels their books and toys. It was quite a serious business, the final packing up of their property.

This was their first introduction to the realities of life, and very important they felt themselves on the occasion. Earnest and hot they became, too, as their labours went on, for some of the packages were anything but accommodating, and permitted their contents to push holes through the paper in which they were wrapped. Still they were very happy in their employment; for what children of their age are not charmed with the prospect of moving to a new place?

"I wonder what Aunt Milicent's house is like," remarked Edith, as she busied herself with her work: "I daresay it is very different to what I imagine."

"I don't care much about the house," said Maud; "I shouldn't wonder if it's a pokey little place; but that won't signify. Any sort of house does well enough to live in, if there's a nice large fruit garden, with plenty of apple and pear trees, so that one can climb up and feast on the fruit."

"And make yourself ill," answered Edith.

"*Ill!* as if apples and pears would make me ill! I'm not afraid of *that*. Anyhow, I hope we shall have some fun when we *are* at Riversdale. It will be much nicer living in the country than in this horrid great town, where one has to march along the streets as stiff as a poker. I don't care one atom for going out here, except in the garden."

"I think we have quite finished our work now," said Edith, looking with satisfaction at the neat parcels; "but perhaps it would be best to write on those we intend to give away as presents, or there may be some mistake after all our trouble." And she wrote in a clear round hand the different names of those for whom the gifts were meant.

Just then the clock struck two. Edith reminded her sister they must lose no time if they wished to take leave of old John and Bridget. So, hurrying as fast as they could, they made their way to the gardener's cottage, and presented the gifts they had so carefully worked during Maud's illness. A kettle holder, Edith's present, and a needle book from Maud, were duly admired by Bridget, who resolved then and there that the holder should be hung up by the side of the fireplace, and never on no account used, but kept as an ornament, whilst the needle book would come in handy most days, and never fail to remind her of the dear young lady whose gift it was. Old John, too, hearing the children's voices, left his work close by, and came into the cottage. He was greatly pleased with the kind thought bestowed on him by the little girls, who each gave him a book mark.

"Mind you, missie," he said, turning to Edith, "it don't require nothing like this yer to keep you and Miss Maud in remembrance. It will be terrible dull never to see you running about the garden, nor hear your young voices a calling out for John to do this thing or that. I don't hold with the captain a going out to them furrin parts: much better bide with them that knows how to value him and his lady. Howsomever, I suppose it must be, and I only hope we may be spared to see them safe back in Old England."

"Yes, John, I hope so," said Edith. "And now, Maud, say good-bye, for we must make haste back to nurse." And the little girls ran quickly down the long gravel path to the house, whilst John and his wife watched their retreating figures until they were quite out of sight.

The children found the carriage at the door, and nurse anxiously waiting to take them to the station, which they reached in a very short time. Quickly the little party in the railway carriage were carried away farther and farther from the large town of B——. The novelty of travelling amused them for some considerable time; but as hour after hour went by, they began to hope their journey would soon come to an end, and though too light-hearted to care for slight inconveniences, yet they were very pleased when they reached Riversdale.

It was late in the evening when they drove up to their new home, so they could only see a dingy-looking house, (as they thought,) and a servant standing at the door. Then they saw a tall slight lady walking across the hall to meet them. They knew this must be their aunt.

"Welcome to Riversdale, my dear children," said Aunt Milicent, in a very kind voice. "I am sure you must be tired and hungry after your long journey. Come with me." And Miss Campbell took them into a sitting-room, which looked bright and cheerful; but the best sight of all to the young travellers was the well-spread dining-table.

A substantial tea of cold meat, hot mashed potatoes, and fruit, had been prepared for them by Aunt Milicent's thoughtfulness. Miss Campbell did not say much to the children that night; she thought they would be glad of rest after all the fatigue they had gone through. She only expressed a hope that they would be happy during the time they remained at Riversdale, and was glad to think they would still have their kind, good nurse with them.

The two girls were pleased to find they were to share the same room, having always done so hitherto. Their beds were not far apart, and when nurse left them for the night, they had a long chat over the events of the day, until Edith declared she could keep awake no longer; and Maud, finding every question she asked her received no answer, followed her sister's example by soon falling asleep.

The children felt very strange when they awoke next morning, and could not for a minute or so recollect where they were. When they did, it was with rather a feeling of fear as to what the future might prove. Whilst they were talking nurse came in to tell them they must get up at once, as the breakfast bell would shortly ring, so they quickly dressed, with her help, anxious to be in good time. On entering the breakfast room they found their aunt was not there. Whilst waiting for her, Maud began peeping about, to see what was on the table. Soon she saw two plates of bread and butter.

"Edith," she said, "just come here and see what is put all ready for us. I declare I never saw such bread and scrape. I wonder if we are *always* going to have this kind of thing! Horrid stuff! No more nice hot toast for us, I expect, like dear old nursie gave us on Sundays and her birthdays, which came so often in the year."

"Maud, Maud, do be careful what you are saying. If auntie should come into the room, and hear you make such rude remarks, I don't know what she would say. Come and sit down quietly with me."

"I am not going to do any such thing," replied the little girl. "I want to see everything I can."

Whilst Edith was trying to silence her sister, Miss Campbell entered the room. She kissed each of her nieces warmly, inquiring if they had slept well, and bidding them take their seats at the table, poured out the coffee.

Maud's fears were realized as to the fare they would have at breakfast, but notwithstanding it was only plain bread and butter, she managed to get through several slices. She remained very silent during the whole of breakfast time, quite out of temper, and was not sorry when Miss Campbell gave them permission to go into the garden.

Alone with her sister, Maud began to grumble at the breakfast they had had.

"I declare," she said, "I don't feel fit to do anything. I only hope Aunt Milicent does not intend our beginning lessons for some days. I can plainly see what it will be, living here; we shall be kept as strict and as miserable as possible."

"Would you rather go to school at once?" asked Edith.

"Yes," replied Maud, "much rather. We should not be cooped up at school in the same way as we shall be at Riversdale; besides, *there* we should have some fun with our school-fellows; but with auntie it will be nothing but lessons, lessons, from morning till night."

"Oh, Maud, you are put out, and determined to think Aunt Milicent will make it wretched for us. I am sure she seems very kind."

"Well, all I know is," continued Maud, "I shall be certain to get into scrapes, and I don't care if I do."

How much longer this state of things might have gone on it would be difficult to say, for Maud's anger waxed hotter and hotter, had not Edith interrupted her by saying, "I hear Aunt Milicent calling us;" and she ran off, leaving the much-injured Maud to follow.

During the first week the children were allowed to do much as they pleased in the way of play, but at the expiration of that time their aunt said they must commence their studies. The morning they were to begin their lessons, Miss Campbell took them into a pleasant, cheerful room, the window of which opened out upon the lawn. In summer the view from this side of the house was very pretty: one could see across the fields and down the green lanes. The walls were covered with ivy and climbing roses; and as the house stood on rising ground, it would perhaps have been too sunny, had not some beautiful old trees cast a pleasant shade over it in the middle of the day.

"This, my dears," said Aunt Milicent, "will be your school-room whilst you are here, and I hope you will both do your best to improve, by being attentive at your studies during the few months you are with me before going to school. I will now just ascertain how far advanced you are."

Maud stood looking very glum; she disliked being catechized, (as she called it,) and although she was a very clever child, it was only a few of her lessons she could endure.

"Are you fond of music, my dears?" asked Miss Campbell.

"I am not fond of *anything*," Maud hastened to reply.

"I am, auntie," said Edith, "and mamma is so anxious for me to get on with it. I hope you will allow me to practice every day."

"Yes, my dear child, you shall certainly do so. I remember now, your mamma, when writing to me, said you had a nice touch and correct ear. Perhaps music is your especial talent, Edith: a very pleasant one it is. But we must remember that we each have to account for talents entrusted to our care. We must not be vain of them, or merely use them for our own gratification. I am sorry Maud does not care for music, too; however, without having any particular taste for it, she may learn to play very tolerably if she has perseverance."

"But, Aunt Milicent," said Edith, "Maud can play several very pretty pieces, and numbers of Czerny's Exercises. She is fond of reading, too, although she does not say so."

"What kind of reading?" inquired Miss Campbell.

"Story books," replied Maud, quickly.

Her aunt did not appear surprised at this.

"I was much the same when I was a little girl," she said. "You will, then, I hope, enjoy History, which is quite as interesting as many tales."

Maud looked up, and said, archly, "Oh yes, that it is. I mean all those parts like the history of the two little princes who were murdered in the tower; or the story about King Charles, who tried to make his escape from Carisbrook Castle, in the Isle of Wight. What a pity he was discovered in the attempt. Last summer mamma took Edith and me to Carisbrook, and we saw the very window he tried to get out of. But I think I most enjoy reading about fair Rosamond's bower, and that wicked Queen Eleanor finding her way by means of the silken thread, and taking the poison and dagger, to make Rosamond choose by which death she would die. I only wish Queen Eleanor had been made to drink the poison herself; she richly deserved it."

"I think," observed Aunt Milicent, smiling, when the little girl paused, "that you have a very good memory, and your love of reading may prove a great help to you in many ways."

"But, auntie," said Maud, and she shrugged her shoulders, "reading history is very different to learning it. When it comes to remembering all the dry parts, and repeating the horrid dates, why then I *hate* it. Who cares about William the Conqueror having the curfew bell rung at any particular hour; or William Rufus and the colour of his hair? Much better to forget that it *was* a hideous red."

Edith could not help laughing, and Miss Campbell said, "You must not expect, Maud, only to have what you consider pleasant in learning. You would not wish to be unlike others of your own age, and remain ignorant."

"Well, all I know is," said Maud, "I don't care to be plagued with lessons."

Notwithstanding Miss Maud's opinion, she, as well as Edith, had to read both French and English to their aunt. Music followed, Edith showing considerable talent, playing several pieces with good execution and taste. Maud, too, managed to get through some tunes and exercises, to Miss Campbell's satisfaction.

Having gone so far, their aunt said, "And now, my dears, the only thing I will ask you to do this morning is to write a copy, whilst I go and see some poor people who are waiting for me in the hall."

Edith set to work most diligently, taking great pains to write her copy well. Maud at first was steady, but before her task was half finished, became tired of it, and commenced drawing pictures of animals, "Trusty," her favourite dog, being very conspicuous amongst the number. Every now and then Edith heard her sister remarking, with satisfaction, "Capital, just like the dear old dog."

"Maud, what are you doing?"

"Come over here, my dear, and you will see," replied the idle child. "I am following the advice given me at the top of my copy, which says, 'Waste not, want not,' and really I have not wasted an inch of paper, but have well filled it up. Aunt Milicent cannot complain of my being extravagant. But do be quick, for I have yet three more lines of this tiresome copy to write before I have done with it."

Edith, however, did not do as she was requested, for at that moment the door opened, and their aunt entered the room.

"Edith," said Miss Campbell, when she had taken a seat, "bring me your copy."

On being examined it was pronounced well and neatly done, and Edith, by her aunt's direction, put it away with the rest of her books.

"Come, Maud, why are you so long over your writing?" asked Aunt Milicent.

Maud coloured, not knowing what answer to make to this question; but taking up her copy-book, walked very slowly across the room, and put it into her aunt's hand without saying a word. It did not take long to see what the little girl had done. Slowly and deliberately Miss Campbell tore out the offending page, and threw it into the fire. Maud's face grew crimson, but she said nothing, only held her hands tightly locked together, to prevent any word escaping.

"Maud," said Miss Campbell, gravely, "I am astonished at your bringing me your book in this disgraceful state. It must be written over again. I cannot allow you to be careless and giddy when at your studies. This afternoon I had intended taking you both with me to call at Summerleigh Manor, and make the acquaintance of the little Grahams. Now, instead of doing so, you will remain at home."

Maud looked down; she was really sorry for having vexed her aunt, and sorry, too, to think that through her own fault she and Edith had forfeited the pleasure they might otherwise have had. On being left alone, Maud set to work, and in the course of half an hour was able to show Miss Campbell a neatly written copy.

CHAPTER III.

Up to Mischief again.

Summerleigh Manor was not more than half a mile from Riversdale; it was a large rambling house, built many years ago. The granite walls looked as though they might well last another century. It lay down in a hollow, almost hidden among the trees; but at one end there was a turret, and from this turret could be seen the country for many miles round. Mr. and Mrs. Graham, with their three children, had lately come from Scotland, and taken possession of the old place, which for some time had been untenanted. The garden was a complete wilderness, which the young people seemed to think much nicer than if it was in order, for they could run about in every direction without fear of doing mischief. Very sorry they were when one day they saw Alick the gardener taking a survey, to see what could be done to make it a little more "ship-shape," as he expressed it.

But now my readers will be anxious to hear something about the children introduced in this chapter. Harold, the eldest, a boy of twelve, was a generous, noble-hearted lad, full of life and spirits, rather difficult to manage in some respects, and certainly more partial to play than study. Wilfrid was three years younger than his brother; then came little Ethel, just five, the darling and pet of the whole house. The boys were devoted to their sister, and did not consider their happiness complete unless she shared their pleasures with them.

The Grahams had heard of the arrival of Edith and Maud at Riversdale, and were anxious to make their acquaintance; for, as Harold had observed on several occasions, he was sure they were awfully jolly. It would be nice to know them, as they lived so near, and would be able to come and play.

One afternoon, whilst amusing themselves in the garden, Wilfrid saw Miss Campbell and the two girls walking up the carriage drive to the front door, so he and Harold waited about, thinking perhaps they might be sent for. Very disappointed they were when, after a short time, they caught sight of all three disappearing down the road.

"What a bother!" exclaimed Harold; "we shall never know them. What's to be done, old fellow?"

"Why," replied Wilfrid, "ask mother to invite them to spend an afternoon with us."

"All right," said Harold, "I'll go at once and make the request." And off he scampered helter skelter. In a few minutes he returned, throwing his cap up in the air, and shouting, "The victory's won, and mother has promised to invite them next Saturday."

The morning after the Hamiltons' visit to Summerleigh Manor, whilst the two girls were at their studies, a note was handed to Miss Campbell by the servant. Having read it, she left the room, telling them to learn the lessons she had marked during her absence. No sooner was the door shut, and Miss Campbell safely gone, than Maud began.

"Edith, don't you wish we could be quite grown up all at once? Then we should have no lessons to learn, but just do whatever we pleased."

"Don't go on talking, Maud; you won't know your French and History when auntie comes back."

"I *must* speak sometimes," replied the little chatterbox; "but if *you* wish to keep silence, I'll talk to myself. Dear me," she continued, "how tired I am of learning; we are at it from morning till night. Well, I'll try and get through this horrid geography first. I hope auntie has marked me sufficient for one morning! What a list of names! enough to make one stammer! I can't bear the sight of a map. I wish all the places had never been found out; then, at least, we should have had one lesson less to learn. Now, French I don't mind; that's a comfort, so I'll keep it until the last. Ah, but what's *this*, placed so nicely underneath my French book? Spelling, I declare! I'm quite sure if I went on learning till midnight I could never remember such a heap of words. Of course it's quite impossible, so there's an end of it." And she closed the book, throwing it down with no little violence.

In the course of an hour Miss Campbell entered the room.

"Come, children," she said, "and say your lessons; you have had plenty of time to learn them."

Edith's were perfectly repeated; but Maud made a sad attempt when her turn came, and was desired to remain in the schoolroom the whole afternoon, until she had committed them to memory, instead of playing in the garden as usual.

In the evening Aunt Milicent told the children she had received a note from Mrs. Graham, asking her to allow them to spend the following Saturday afternoon at the Manor House.

"And may we go, auntie?" asked Edith.

"Well, my dear, I should like you to know the little Grahams, for I think they are nice children. Harold is your age, Edith, and the second boy nine, just a year younger than Maud. I intend you both to go, that is to say, if I find Maud really trying to be steady and diligent with her lessons. If she is not, then she must remain at home, and I shall let Mrs. Graham know the reason she does not go with you."

Maud looked somewhat crestfallen, and remained very quiet; but in a short time she began, when alone with Edith, talking about Summerleigh Manor, wondering what their new friends would be like. Very careful she was, too, for the next few days to attend to her studies, and when Friday morning's lessons were finished satisfactorily, felt quite sure that all would be right for her the next day.

As there was a heavy downpour of rain, and no getting out, the children amused themselves during the evening in the schoolroom. Nurse, who had come in, was made to take the most comfortable chair they could find, and listen to all they had to tell her.

At last she said, "Well now, Miss Maud, your tongue has been rattling along for an hour. I feels quite dizzy like with the constant buzzing in my ears. Can't you no ways manage to keep quiet?"

"Yes, nurse, I'll keep quiet," replied Maud, "if you and Edith do so."

"I don't fancy Miss Edith will mind a little less noise, bless her! if she only haves a book to look at; and I shall be happy enough with mine, with the fine large print, and my specs to help me."

"I'll settle all that," said Maud. And away she ran in search of the glasses, soon bringing them to nurse, with the book mentioned; and then handing Edith her "Fairy Tales," she was left to her own devices.

"Dear me," she said, sitting down, and looking at the clock, "it's only seven; there's one whole hour before bed-time. I must think of something to do, and what shall that be? Ah, I know what would be great fun,—just to sew dear old nursie into her chair, and watch her trying to get up with it safely fixed on to her. Yes, I'll do that."

Walking quietly on tip-toe, Maud went to

the table on which was Nurse Grey's work-basket, and helping herself to needle, cotton, and scissors, returned noiselessly, seating herself immediately behind nurse. "Now," she thought, "there's no time to be lost;" and she stitched away until she had fastened the poor woman's dress to the chair at least in half a dozen places. Once or twice she could not help giving a little laugh as she thought of the mischief she was doing so successfully, causing nurse to look off her book, and say:

"Miss Maud, don't be giving way to idleness, but go on with your work; may be you will finish the hem of your aunt's pocket-handkerchief this evening, and for once in a way have passed the time usefully."

"I'm busy enough, nurse," answered the mischievous child. "Don't let me interrupt your reading."

"That's something like thought for you to say, my dear. As it wants ten minutes to eight, I may as well read on to the end of this chapter, for it's mighty interesting, I can tell you."

Nurse being once again absorbed with her book, Maud resolved to hide behind the window curtain, and wait until a move was made by her victim. She had only time to do this when Nurse Grey closed her book, saying:

"Come, my dears, it's bed-time now; but you've been that good this evening, quite out of the common, it almost made me forget the hour. Bless me, whatever's the matter?" she said, trying to rise. "I don't seem able to move." A second attempt was made, but with no better success. "Well, to be sure, I can't get rid of this chair no way. For pity's sake, Miss Edith, come and give a look."

Edith did as she was requested, and at first could not speak for laughing.

Nurse was much vexed at Edith's ill-timed mirth, saying: "Miss Maud's been up to some of her tricks, I suppose; it's downright shameful, that it is. As to you, Miss Edith, I'm astonished at you a laughing; I never expected to see you encouraging such ways."

"I'm sorry I have vexed you," said Edith, when she saw how annoyed the old woman was; "but you do look so funny, I couldn't help laughing. Shall I get the scissors and cut the stitches?"

"Yes, my dear, pray do." And Nurse Grey appeared somewhat pacified with Edith's apology. "Bless me, how much more is there to undo?" she asked, as Edith continued the work.

"Only two more places, nurse; I shall soon finish."

Maud now began to feel a little uncomfortable

at the result of her mischief, and thinking she had better keep out of sight altogether, managed to slip unperceived from behind the curtain, and into a cupboard in the bedroom.

When nurse was freed from the chair she shook her dress in high dudgeon at seeing the rumpled condition it was in, telling Edith to come off to bed at once.

"What can have become of Maud, nurse?"

"I don't know, missie, and I ain't going to waste another moment's thought on her this night. To-morrow I shall make known to your aunt how badly she has behaved, as it is my duty so to do."

"I am afraid auntie will not allow her to go to Summerleigh Manor when she hears it," said Edith, with a sigh.

"I don't doubt it, my dear; howsomever, if she ain't cured of them ways now, she never will be."

Edith soon got into bed, and nurse went downstairs to her supper. When all was quiet, Edith thought she heard some one moving, and looking round, saw her sister coming out of the cupboard. "Maud," she exclaimed, "what have you done?"

"You know well enough," was the reply. "The question is, what am I to do? Nurse is in a fine rage, and will get me into trouble if she tells Aunt Milicent. I think I'll be quick and write a nice coaxing little note, asking her to forgive me; yes, that will be best."

In a few minutes the culprit was undressed, and perched up in bed, writing the following appeal:

"Dearest Nursie,

"Will you be so very kind as to forgive me just this once, and not tell Aunt Milicent? I promise not to play any more tricks for a long time. I am in bed, and feeling so sad, in case you keep angry: so please do as I ask.

"Maud."

Having folded it up, she placed it in a conspicuous place, and wishing Edith good-night, was soon fast asleep.

When Nurse Grey came into the room, shortly after her supper, she caught sight of the note. On reading the contents, the old woman smiled, and stooping down, kissed the little girl, saying, "Bless her! I couldn't have the heart to say a word against the dear lamb. She looks so innocent like, lying there, no one would never believe she could be up to such ways. Well, I suppose it's no use my keeping stern any longer. I must give her a bit of my mind to-morrow for duty's sake, and then let it pass."

The next morning Maud received very meekly the lecture nurse thought necessary to give, congratulating herself on getting off so easily.

At four o'clock that afternoon Edith and Maud went to Summerleigh Manor. As they entered the house they heard the merry voices of children. Mrs. Graham welcomed them very kindly, and after talking for a short time, took them upstairs, where Harold, with Wilfrid and Ethel, were in the midst of their play. It did not take long for them to get on friendly terms, and then came the important question as to what games they should have. "Hide-and-seek" was decided on. Maud and Harold were to hide first, and marched off down some long passages, until they reached a large lumber room. It was rather dark, the shutters being only partly opened. After climbing over a number of boxes, Harold pointed out an immense cupboard.

"You will not mind getting in here?" he said; "it's a jolly place."

Maud *did* mind very much, but thought it would not do to say so.

"I'm quite ready," she replied, "only how can I manage to get up so high?"

"Well, that's the puzzle," said Harold; "you are so dreadfully small."

"Yes, I know I am," answered Maud, with a

sigh; "and it's very tiresome when one is wanted for this sort of thing. But perhaps I can do it if you will get in first and drag me up."

Harold, after one or two attempts, landed himself safely into the cupboard.

"Hurrah! it's splendid," he said. "Come on as fast as you can; the others will be tired of waiting."

Maud felt she must go through it; Harold would think her so stupid if she refused. But alas! when half way up she fell with a hard bump on the floor. Tears came into her eyes, for she had struck her knee against the sharp edge of a box, causing her great pain. Harold, meanwhile, was sitting comfortably, laughing at his friend's misfortune.

"Never mind," he said, "try again. I'm glad to see you don't make a fuss over a few knocks, like most girls would."

Maud was pleased at this remark, and fortunately succeeded in her second attempt in getting into the cupboard. There was only just time to close the door when they heard Wilfrid entering the room, saying to his companions, "Now this shall be the very last place we will look for them." Having given a hasty search, he and Edith decided on giving it up, and going into the garden until the others joined them.

UP TO MISCHIEF AGAIN. 39

Harold and Maud sat for some time in their hiding place, talking over plans they hoped to carry out when the midsummer holidays came round. At length Harold suggested they should get down, as it must be near tea-time. He quickly managed to lower himself, but with poor Maud it was not quite so easy a matter. It seemed as if she never could get down from such a height. At last Harold remembered seeing some steps on a landing close by, and having brought them in, and placed them firmly against the wall, the little girl descended in safety.

"My goodness me, you *are* a sight," he exclaimed, "covered with dust and dirt."

"Oh dear, what shall I do?" said Maud. "I cannot go before Mrs. Graham such a dreadful figure. Can't you make me look a little better?"

"All right," he answered, good-naturedly, "if I rub you down a bit you'll do very well; besides, I remember that, as good luck will have it, we are to have tea by ourselves, so you need not bother about your dress."

"I am glad of that," said Maud, greatly relieved.

Making their way downstairs and into the garden, where they found their companions, Harold was called upon to give an account of the last hour, and amused them with a description of Maud's unlucky tumble.

"Well," said Wilfrid, "all I can say is, that you won't catch me playing at 'hide-and-seek' again. I don't see the fun of your being shut up all the afternoon by yourselves."

Whilst this discussion was going on a servant came to tell them the tea was ready. A merry party they were seated round the table. Edith was requested to take what was considered the seat of honour, *i.e.*, to pour out the tea, Harold and Wilfrid making themselves useful by cutting the cakes, and attending to the wants of their visitors. Maud, as usual, was busy with her tongue, asking her newly-made friends no end of questions. Once or twice Edith, fearing her sister was becoming too inquisitive, shook her head at her when she thought the others were not looking; but it was all in vain. Maud continued just the same.

The rest of the evening was passed by the children in various games, and very sorry they were when told that Nurse Grey was waiting to take Edith and Maud home.

CHAPTER IV.

Maud's Birthday.—The Picnic at Seaforth.

"Maud," said Miss Campbell one evening to her little niece, "Edith tells me that your birthday is on the 14th of September, which will be next Tuesday. I was thinking you might enjoy a picnic with some of your young friends. Do you think that would be a pleasant way of passing the day?"

"Oh, auntie, that would be beautiful; I should like it above everything. But, Aunt Milicent, who shall we invite, and where shall we go?"

"Well, my dear, I do not think you know many children."

"No," replied Maud, "*dreadfully* few; but those we do know are worth a heap of others. Shall I just say the names of all those I can remember?"

"By all means," said Miss Campbell.

So Maud commenced: "Of course Harold comes first, then Wilfrid. Ethel is *rather* young, but I suppose we must do our best to look after her, and see she does not get into mischief. And, auntie, do you think we might invite Dora and Katie Leslie; they are so nice. Then there is Frank Willoughby; if he came, too, it would be capital. I don't believe we should care to have any more, even if we *could* choose, should we, Edith?"

Edith had been patiently listening to the list of friends, but when questioned, said, " I think if auntie would allow us to invite Helen Murray it would be a great pleasure to her, as well as to ourselves; but perhaps too many have been invited already."

"No, my dear, not at all," said Miss Campbell; "I am quite willing that Helen should come. And now we have decided who are to be of the party, the next matter for consideration is, *where* shall we go? As you are strangers, I will fix on a place; and as I think you would enjoy the seaside, we will go to the pretty little village of Seaforth, some fifteen miles from here."

"Oh, Aunt Milicent," exclaimed Maud, in delight, "I think my next birthday will be the very nicest I shall ever have had all my life. Edith, don't you long for yours?"

"I shall have to wait some months for mine," replied Edith, despondingly.

"Never mind," said Miss Campbell; "when

it does come we will have some pleasure, I hope, that will mark the day. But now I think you must begin to write your notes of invitation. I shall have the *substantial* part of the business to look after, and see that there is plenty of food provided for all the hungry little folks on the occasion. I think there will be ten or twelve, without counting 'Trusty,' who will most certainly expect his share."

"Dear old faithful 'Trusty,'" said Edith; "I don't think we should be quite happy if he did not go with us."

Their aunt having supplied them with writing materials, was leaving the room, when Maud said: "Please, auntie, *must* we write them all ourselves? It will take such a long time."

"You must do your best," replied Miss Campbell; "it will not do for you always to depend on others for everything you need; so begin at once."

Maud shook her head, and gave a deep sigh, but knew it would be useless to say anything more; so the two children began their work in good earnest. Some time passed, and much to their satisfaction, before they went to bed that night all the notes were finished, with the exception of three, which they hoped to write the next day.

"Will you read those we have written, auntie?" asked Maud.

"I can only look at one or two," replied Miss Campbell, "for I see it is a quarter to nine, and nurse will be in a state of mind at your being up so late."

Maud selected what she considered the most important note for her aunt to read first. It was with some difficulty Miss Campbell managed to keep grave as her eyes fell on the little girl's production.

"My dear Harold,

"We are to have a beautiful picnic to Seaforth next Tuesday, as it will be my birthday. Aunt Milicent has given me permission to ask lots of my friends, so I think we shall have capital fun. I believe there are numbers of rocks and splendid places for climbing at Seaforth, just what you will enjoy. I hope you will be able to come early. I think we shall start from here by eleven o'clock. Mind you bring some of your fishing rods, as we shall have a good chance of making use of them. Give my love to Wilfrid and Ethel; of course this invitation is meant for them too. I hope you will answer this note soon; I shall be so anxious to hear from you. Don't you long for Tuesday to come? I do. I can't write more, as I have to finish two more notes, so good bye.

"Your very affectionate friend,
"MAUD HAMILTON.

"P.S.—Please don't notice the blots I have made. I haven't time to write the note again."

Maud stood by, watching Miss Campbell's face very anxiously, and was delighted when no fault was found. Certainly there could be no mistake as to the person for whom the letter was intended, as the little girl had directed the envelope in writing large enough to be read at some distance off.

"Just look, auntie," she said, as she ran to the door with it in her hand; "even where I am standing you can see who it's meant for. I was quite determined Harold should not lose his invitation from the address not being quite plain. I have often noticed how the postman goes on looking at his packet of letters, as if he cannot read very well; but now there can be no excuse."

"At all events, Maud, he will not require spectacles to read this one. And now I will read one of Edith's notes, after which you must go off to bed."

"Bless me," exclaimed Nurse Grey the next morning, "if this ain't the third time I've called them children. I believe if the chimney pots was to fall through the roof it wouldn't do much to wake them; it's always the case when their aunt keeps them up to such late hours. I'll just give them a bit of a shake." Saying this, nurse went up to Maud's bed, calling in a loud voice, "Come, come, missie, do you intend sleeping all day? It's near eight o'clock. Do you hear what I say?"

Maud began rubbing her eyes, and, sitting up, inquired if anything was the matter.

"Anything the matter, indeed!" nurse replied. "All I can say is, if you want any breakfast you'd better be quick."

The conversation awoke Edith, who, hearing how late it was, jumped up, and in a short time both she and Maud were dressed, and ran downstairs to the breakfast room.

The children found it rather difficult to give their attention to anything in the way of studies that morning. Maud declared her fingers would not play properly, and even Edith made an unusual number of mistakes with her music, so much were their thoughts occupied with the coming picnic. Very delighted they were when Miss Campbell said they should have the afternoon free to finish the invitations, so that they could be sent to the post that evening.

Tuesday came at last. Maud awoke quite early, and the first thing she saw on a table by her bed was a workbox nicely fitted up, a present from her aunt. Very pleased she was with the useful and pretty gift. A small parcel, directed in Edith's writing, proved to be a box of colours.

"Ah," said the little girl, as she looked at the contents with satisfaction, "I'm glad Edith has chosen this: it is just what I was in want of; my old box is nearly done for. But what can *this* be?" she added, taking up a brown paper packet. "A book! and what a beauty! Let me see what the title is,—'The Castaways.' The very book I have longed to have. Well, I must wake up that lazy Edith at once." Suiting the action to the word, Maud ran over to her sister, whom she soon succeeded in rousing. "Edith, *do* come and sit on my bed," she said; "I want you to look at all my presents." Having made themselves comfortable, they inspected the treasures.

"What a nice workbox," remarked Edith; "and a silver thimble, too."

"Yes, I do admire it," replied her sister; "but you have not seen this beautiful book, one I've often wished to read. I know Harold has it, for he told me it was awfully interesting. I just took a peep at it, and saw something about boys and girls being shipwrecked and cast upon a desert island. Won't it be a treat for us, when we have a quiet time, to enjoy a good long spell of reading?"

"Well, Maud, this birthday of yours I call a *splendid* one."

"Yes, that it is," answered her sister, "and I'm so happy. Do you think before we begin to dress there will be time to look at the pictures in the book? I know there are several. I wish I could find out who has given it to me."

And now, seated side by side, they admired the pretty illustrations, which in some measure told them of the chief events mentioned in the story. Presently a piece of paper dropped out from one of the leaves Maud was turning over, on which was written: "For dear Miss Maud, from Nurse Grey, wishing her very many happy returns of the day."

"How kind of that dear old nursie," exclaimed Maud; "fancy her giving me such a handsome present. Won't I hug and kiss her a hundred times; and I believe I hear her coming upstairs now. Yes, here she is."

"Good morning, my dears," said Nurse Grey on entering the room.

Maud sprang off the bed, and catching nurse

round the neck, declared she deserved to be kissed to death. And by the manner in which the old woman was attacked it did not seem likely she would live long.

Having unfastened Maud's firmly-clasped arms, and regained her somewhat lost breath, she said, "Lor, missie, you've nearly done for me. I never thought to find you so lively like, the first thing in the morning. If the outside of the book makes you so dreadful wild, whatever will you be when you comes to the reading part? You'll be almost dangerous, with them wild spirits of yours. But come, my dears, be quick, or you'll be behindhand, which won't do, considering all that has to be done to-day."

When the two little girls went downstairs there was no one in the breakfast room, so Maud rushed to the window to look for the postman just in time to see him coming towards the house. He handed her a number of letters, three of which were directed to "Miss Maud Hamilton."

"Oh, my!" she said; "fancy my having three, and such big ones, too! How nice it is having a birthday. I should like twenty every year."

Before breakfast was ready Maud had time to read them through. One was from Harold Graham, wishing his little friend many happy returns of the day, and saying he had a present of a fishing rod, which he intended giving her when they met at the picnic.

"That's *very* thoughtful of Harold," observed Maud, "and it's just as well to know how to do everything oneself. If ever I am cast upon a desert island, (and somehow I always fancy that *will* be my fate,) I may have to live on all the fish I can catch, so I had better learn whilst I have the opportunity."

Aunt Milicent listened to these remarks much amused, but said nothing.

"I hope I shall never be shipwrecked with you," said Edith, "for I don't look forward to living on some lonely, wretched place, as *you* do; and as to living on the fish *you* caught, I fancy one would go on rather short commons."

"What nonsense you talk," replied Maud; "don't you understand? I am going to be taught how to fish properly, so you would be well supplied. But now we will see what Helen Murray's note says."

The answer to Maud's invitation was very satisfactory. Helen was delighted with the idea of spending some hours at the seaside.

The third letter was a curiosity of penmanship, from old John the gardener, who said, "He minded well as how it was Miss Maud's birthday. He'd been a thinking of it for some weeks past. His missus had been working downright hard to get the book-mark finished in time, and they hoped that little miss wouldn't be above accepting such a trifle." The epistle ended by sending their duty to all inquiring friends.

"Poor old John," said Maud; "it is very good of him to remember me. But now, auntie, I must not keep you any longer, for I see the breakfast is ready."

"Yes, my dear, it is; and we must make haste, too, for there is plenty to be seen to."

Having quickly taken her own breakfast, Miss Campbell left the children to finish theirs, whilst she went to superintend the packing up of the provisions.

It was a merry party that assembled at Riversdale. The Grahams were the first to arrive, Harold carrying a mysterious-looking parcel, which Maud guessed must be the fishing rod and its belongings. She tried to keep her eyes off it, as if she were not too anxious to get possession of the prize. Shortly after the Grahams, the Leslies and others followed. It was decided they should go part of the way by train, and the remainder of the journey in open carriages, which Miss Campbell had engaged for the occasion. It was a gloriously bright morning, not a cloud was in the sky. Harold declared he feared there was no chance of the sea being rough, for there was not a breath of air. The children were in a state of the wildest excitement, and nearly distracted nurse, who appeared to think her responsibilities very heavy, by the way she walked about every now and then, saying, loud enough to be heard, "Bless me, if ever I saw in all my life such a set of madcaps. Miss Maud will be tearing about crazy like, I reckon. Wait till we get to Seaforth, that's all; there'll be no doing nothing with her." These remarks were entirely lost upon the children, whose tongues were rattling as fast as they could go.

It took some minutes to pack them safely in the train, and glad enough Miss Campbell was when they finally started. On reaching the station they found the carriages waiting to take them on to the little village of Seaforth. The drive was thoroughly enjoyed by them. Ethel clapped her hands with delight when she caught sight of the sea; indeed, there was a general feeling of impatience to get down from their seats and make a rush to the water.

"Hurrah! hurrah!" cried the boys, as the carriages stopped. "Here we are at last; how jolly, to be sure." And one after the other sprang down on the road.

"Come, Maud," said Harold, "don't lose a

minute; you have had quite enough of sitting, I should think."

"Yes," she replied; "it's all very pleasant driving along, but rather too quiet for my taste; besides, we hope to do something that will astonish our friends. Just look here," (and she took out of her pocket a large bag;) "I managed to empty all nurse's patch-work; I thought it would do for putting all the fish into that we catch. But I must be sure and take it back, or I shall get a fine scolding."

Harold smiled when he saw the preparations Maud had made, and said, in answer to her anxious look for approval, "I think if we fill half that bag we shall prove ourselves capital hands at fishing."

Whilst they had been talking, the rest of the party had walked on as far as the bench, so Maud and Harold ran to see how their companions were amusing themselves. They found Ethel busily engaged in building a sand house, and great was the child's delight as she saw it gradually getting higher and higher; whilst the others were employed in various ways.

"Don't you think, Harold," whispered Maud, "that this would be a good time for us to be off? Aunt Milicent and Mrs. Graham are talking together under that cliff. What do you say?"

"Perhaps it may be the best chance we shall have," he replied; "but it must be twelve o'clock, and we should miss our dinner; and to tell you the truth, I am getting awfully hungry."

"Surely you won't wait for dinner?" said Maud, in a tone of surprise. "Who knows, if we are not quick about it, something may happen to stop our expedition altogether. As to dinner, if you will promise to wait here until I return, I'll settle *that* matter."

"All right," replied Harold, as he stretched himself on the beach, and watched his little friend, as she flew along, bent on securing something from the store of provisions she knew nurse had in her charge.

As Maud reached the place Miss Campbell had selected as being the most suitable for spreading the cloth for dinner, nurse was not to be seen. In all probability she had gone to one of the fishermen's cottages to ask for water. Maud stood looking at the eatables which had been taken out of the hamper. Amongst the things was a tempting-looking meat pie. "Ah," she thought, "that would be just the very thing for Harold, as he is so hungry, if nurse would only be coaxed into giving some of it." She became tired of standing, and impatient at the delay, so, taking a seat close to the pie, thought she would see what it was made of. With the help of a knife she managed to raise the crust without breaking it, and, delighted at her success, laid it carefully down on a plate. "Now then," she said, "I must taste it;" and taking a mouthful, found it extremely good. "Chicken and ham; just the nicest thing one could have." A second piece was taken. "Better still," thought Maud; "but I suppose I must not carry it all away. Oh, here comes nurse; I'll see what I can do with her." And replacing the pie-crust, she ran to meet her. "Nursie, dear," she said, in a coaxing voice, "I've such a favour to ask, and as it is my birthday I don't think you will have the heart to say no."

"Well, my darling," replied Nurse Grey, smiling, "if it is anything in my power I won't deny you. What is it you want?"

"You can do it quite well, nurse; it is quite an easy thing. I want you just to give me a few things that can be carried without any bother. Harold and I are going on an expedition, and we are *sure* to be hungry before we return; so if you will spare us a meat pie, and one or two small things, like a plum cake and jam tarts, I can put them into a basket."

"An expedition, Miss Maud, that's it, is it? And *where*, may I ask, are you going? It strikes me very forcibly you are after some of your wild schemes, and won't rest content, like the others, but will go on until you get yourself into a world of trouble. Now just listen to me: you'll do no such thing as take a morsel of these yer provisions, not leastways while I have the care of them. If you and Master Harold wants food, come to the proper place to get it; it's no use for you to be talking away your time, for you knows perfectly well that when I says a thing firm like, I'm not to be moved, no more than the rocks we sees yonder. Run away, and make yourself happy with the other young ladies, and get rid of all that nonsense out of your head."

Maud was dreadfully disappointed at her entire failure. What could she do? She knew nurse would not give in when once she was determined. The beautiful plan she had made was quite spoiled.

"You are the very crossest person I ever knew," she said to nurse. "I thought you would have been kind and good-natured for once. I don't care one bit for the picnic, and as to dinner, I'd rather starve than eat any of the things." No notice was taken of this, so she continued, but in an altered tone of voice, "If you would only just do this one little thing you would make us so happy."

"If you was to stand there a month, missie,

I wouldn't give you a crumb to encourage you in such ways; so now you understand me, I hope."

"Horrid old crosspatch! that's what nurse is to-day," muttered Maud, as she walked off. "What will Harold say to my returning empty-handed? I must tell him in the best way I can."

"Well," inquired Harold, "what have you secured after being away so long? something worth having, I trust."

Maud looked very crestfallen as she related her unsuccessful appeal to nurse. Harold, although he did not say so, felt considerably relieved when he heard how matters had ended.

"Never mind," he said; "it will be much the best way for us to dine with the others, and make our escape later on. It would look rude if we did not appear, especially as the party is *yours.*"

"I suppose it might," she replied. "And now let us go and have some fun until the dinner is ready."

"Oh, here comes Maud," cried Wilfrid, as he saw her running towards them. "Now then, there will be plenty of scampering about, I'll be bound, if she's with us. I say, Maud," he asked, "what on earth have you been about all this time?"

"Very much engaged," was the answer, "*very* busy;" and she looked quite important. "Now I've come to have a game with you all."

"I'm glad of that," said Wilfrid, "for it's awfully slow with them here; I can't get Edith or Dora to do anything, and of course Ethel is too small to be of any use."

"Very well, then," said Maud, "don't lose any time, for we have none to spare. But the question is, what will be the nicest thing for us to do, so that all can play, and then Dora and the others will rouse up? I know," she exclaimed; "such a capital thing I have hit on. You will all agree to it, I hope. What do you say to our taking off our boots and stockings, and having a good dance in the sea? It is beautifully sandy close to the shore. Aunt Milicent would not object, I am sure; for I have often heard her say she wished Edith could bathe her ankles in salt water, it would do them so much good. Come, Ethel, you lazy little thing, bring your spade, and dig a hole in the sand large enough for us to put our boots into. Our stockings we had better tie up in a bundle together, and leave them under these large stones."

Maud's plan was highly approved of, except by Dora, who advised them not to go into the water without permission, and left them to join

THE PICNIC AT SEAFORTH. 59

Helen Murray, who was enjoying a stroll along the beach.

"How stupid of Dora," said Kate Leslie; "she is always prudish in this way. What harm can there be in doing as Maud proposes? However, we shall enjoy ourselves just as much without her."

Having stowed away their boots into the hole Ethel had made in readiness, Maud tied up the stockings; but decided, instead of placing them under the stones, to hang them upon a hook she discovered on one side of a boat-house close by.

"How delicious!" was the exclamation, as the children's hot feet felt the refreshing cool water.

"Dora has missed something by being so foolish," said Maud.

"We must not go too far in," remarked Kate, "for the waves are rather high."

"Don't be a coward," said Wilfrid; "a little salt water can't hurt you. Here, Ethel, give me your hand, and don't stand looking as if you are going to be swallowed up."

Ethel put her hand into her brother's, at the same time feeling rather timid; but in a little time all fear vanished, and she enjoyed the fun as much as any of the elder ones.

CHAPTER V.

Important Events.—Ben Ward's Refusal.

For some time the children remained paddling about, now venturing out a little distance, and then, as a wave almost overtook them, running back to the shore. But of this they became tired, and Maud proposed they should hold each other's hands, and form a circle to have a dance, "just the same," she said, "as if we were playing at 'mulberry bush.'" To this all agreed, and round and round they went, laughing and talking, but not observing that the tide was rapidly rising.

"What fun this is!" exclaimed little Ethel, as she was hurried along by her companions. "Hold me tight, Katie, for my feet hardly touch the ground, you whirl me round so fast."

Scarcely was this said when Maud cried out, "Stop! stop! my goodness me, what are those things swimming about? I do declare all our boots are floating away."

It was only too true. The tide during the last quarter of an hour had reached the spot where the children had placed their boots for safety, and gradually they had been lifted by the waves and carried out into the sea. In the excitement that followed Ethel was left to take care of herself, and whilst they watched the boots slowly but surely taken out of their reach, a large wave unexpectedly swept over them, throwing them with some considerable force to the ground. The sudden shock gave no time for thinking of Ethel, and the poor child was entirely overpowered by it. She gave one long and piercing scream as she was drawn under the water. Edith, seeing the peril she was in, with great presence of mind hurried to her assistance, and was just in time to seize hold of the little girl's frock, thus preventing her from being drawn still further from the shore. It was with the greatest difficulty, however, that she succeeded, with Kate Leslie's help, to carry her back to the beach; even then they could scarcely realize that they were quite out of danger. For a short time Ethel remained with her eyes closed. Anxiously the children watched by her side, Wilfrid in the greatest distress, fearing what might be the result of the accident, kissing his sister, and begging her to speak, if only once, that he might know she was alive. Maud cried bitterly, saying it would be her fault. This scene somewhat changed when, after once or twice shivering all over, the child opened her eyes, and looking round, asked if they were safe.

"Yes, yes," replied Wilfrid, in delight at hearing her voice again, "you are *quite* safe. Don't be frightened; you are not near the water."

"I am so glad," she said, with a sigh of relief. "Wasn't it dreadful? We were nearly drowned, weren't we? And it was so strange, the noise in my ears all the time, just like music. Did you hear it, Wilfrid?"

"No, Ethel; but I was not so long under the water as you were."

"I don't want to play with the sea any more to-day," she said; "I am so cold, and can't keep still." And she trembled from head to foot.

"What had we better do?" asked Kate Leslie. "We must not let her remain like this, she will be ill; we are all in a sad plight, but that little signifies, it's Ethel I'm afraid of."

Whilst they were discussing the question, Mrs. Graham and Miss Campbell, knowing it was time for the children to have their dinner, quitted their seats by the cliffs, and walked towards that part of the beach where they had left the young people at play. Great was their consternation on arriving to find them in such a condition. Fortunately Ethel had wonder-

IMPORTANT EVENTS. 63

fully revived, and was seated up, laughing at the ridiculous sight her companions were with their wet clothes and dripping hair. They felt very uncomfortable as the two ladies came up to them.

"Good gracious me, what is the matter? what have you all been doing?" asked Mrs. Graham.

Ethel made a spring at her mother, saying, "I am quite safe, and Wilfrid and Maud are *so* sorry; please don't be angry with any one, but *do* take me to get some dry clothes, mine are so wet."

Without waiting for any explanation as to how the disaster had occurred, the ladies took Ethel off at once to the nearest cottage, anxious to get rid of her wet garments, leaving the other children to do the best they could for themselves. Left to their own devices, and not being as warm as they could wish, Kate suggested they should run about, as it might perhaps take away the shivers.

"How absurd you are," said Edith: "we cannot possibly do that when we haven't a boot to put on. I wonder where they have sailed to?"

"Why, miles out to sea, I should think," replied Maud, contemptuously. "The boots wouldn't wait to please us while we were staring after them. If we had only made use of our senses we might have called 'Trusty;' he would have fetched them back to the shore safe enough: he's a first-rate dog for the water. But now it's no use our wishing anything at all in the matter: they are gone, never to return; and what we have to do is to acknowledge how it happened, and hope we may get off without punishment."

"The stockings are safe enough," remarked Kate, "that's one good thing; I can see them hanging from here. How the others will laugh at our disaster. I shall walk up and down on that nice smooth piece of sand. Come along, let us all try it: it's so miserable sitting down like this."

Kate's proposition was not a bad one, and they became warmer by moving about, besides the amusement they afforded each other in their attempts to take an occasional run, generally failing, by the sharp stones, which lay concealed under the sand, giving their feet a sudden cut, and causing them to stop and call out loudly. Presently they spied nurse bustling down to the beach, so they quickly seated themselves, covering their feet over to avoid, if possible, her discovering the loss of the boots.

"Young ladies and gentlemen," she said, "why ever don't you come to your dinner?

IMPORTANT EVENTS.

It's near half-past one, and every mortal thing have been on that blessed cloth for the last hour. Depend upon it, if I hadn't got all ready, you'd been up as hungry as wolves, asking for food. Such a beautiful spread as there is, too, fit for any company." The children still remained sitting, which surprised nurse considerably, after all she had said. "You seems inclined to live on this yer beach," continued the old woman; "generally speaking, Miss Maud don't require telling a second time to come to her meals; but perhaps she intends starving to death, as she told me this morning. I can't say I puts much trust in that threat; howsomever, we shall see if it's true or not. Now then, Miss Edith, you come, my dear, and the others will soon follow." As she was saying this, she became aware of the state of their clothes, for although they were almost dry, they looked limp and rumpled. "Mercy me!" exclaimed Nurse Grey, throwing up her hands, "You all look like so many rag bags. I'm certain sure Miss Maud's been up to mischief; I could see it in her face this morning, when she came begging me for pie and tarts."

They now told her about the loss of the boots, laughing heartily at her consternation.

"Did I ever hear of such goings on! And you, Miss Maud, to be making light of it, as if it weren't no ways serious, when you know the untold money as is spent on shoe leather for you and Miss Edith. It's my plain duty to make known to your aunt how you are situated; but it's throwing away breath entirely talking to you, for all I can say don't appear to make no impression." And having said this, Nurse Grey walked herself off.

When she was fairly out of hearing, Wilfrid remarked, "Isn't she up about it? I wish she had stayed away; perhaps we shall get into a row now."

"Oh, no," said Maud; "it's just as well she should tell, and then we shan't have to; and I don't believe we shall get any scolding at all. What do you say, Edith?"

"It will all come right," replied her sister, "if we keep ourselves quiet."

So they sat and chatted on, Maud telling them all she had read about shipwrecks, and how those who had been cast on desert islands lived for years, doing all sorts of wonderful things, until she almost made Wilfrid wish to share the same fate as those mentioned.

"I am not surprised at your longing to be shipwrecked," observed Maud. "It would be a delightful life; no bother with lessons; all the day would be taken up with hunting and fishing. And then there would be the house to build; in fact, we should hardly find time enough to get through all our work. Edith and I will have the best chance, because in a few years we shall be going to India, and then all I have said may come to pass for us. Edith does not seem to enjoy the idea so much as I do, but I am sure she will enjoy it equally well when once she finds herself safe on some beautiful solitary island full of animals and birds; that is what I am longing for." And Maud stopped, quite overcome with the happy thoughts of such a prospect before her.

Whilst listening to this enchanting description, the children had not noticed Mrs. Graham and the others coming down to the beach, nurse carrying Ethel, who was dressed in a most fanciful costume, borrowed from one of the fishermen's wives. The red skirt and blue body gave the little girl a foreign appearance.

"Look at Ethel; she has become an Italian," was the cry.

"We've no money for you, my dear," said Maud, "so you had better go back to your own country." And they laughed, and tried to teaze her, but failed in the attempt, for the object of their mirth enjoyed the fun as much as her would-be tormentors.

"Come, come, children," said Miss Campbell, " do you think you can manage to walk as far as where the dinner is prepared with only your stockings on?"

"Oh, yes," was the ready reply; and with a few knocks and scratches they reached the place, and hungry enough they were. They found Harold with his cousin, Frank Willoughby, impatiently awaiting their arrival, in a state of semi-starvation, declaring they were as hungry as sharks. Certainly they did ample justice to all that was placed before them.

When they had finished their dinner, Miss Campbell said, "Now, my dears, we must consider what can be done to provide you all with boots, or your pleasure will be spoilt for the rest of the day."

"Do you think," suggested Mrs. Graham, "it would do for Harold and Frank to go to the village? They might perhaps succeed in getting something that would answer for the time being."

The boys readily complied, enjoying the commission. Whilst they were gone, Edith was called upon to give an account of the catastrophe. Although they were not scolded for what they had done, the danger was pointed out to them, and the great risk Ethel had run of being drowned, the children listening attentively, really sorry for their thoughtlessness, and promising to be careful in future.

Rather more than half an hour had elapsed when Harold's voice was heard shouting in the distance, as he came scampering along, followed by Frank. "Hurrah! hurrah! we've got them; boots by the million!" Finally reaching the anxious party, Harold threw himself down on the ground by his friend Maud, pretending he was quite exhausted.

"Are we not fortunate," he asked his mother, "in finding such articles? But I declare we had to fish about into the most curious places possible. I happened to catch sight of a pair of boots in a small shop, which contained all the imaginable things one can mention, from pig's trotters to coats, hats, butter, and candles. And such a collection of boots as were brought for our inspection; just what you would like," he said, turning to Maud, "with plenty of nails, and jolly thick soles, which would help to take you over no end of rough places. But I see Mr. Prettyman coming with them, so you can judge for yourselves."

Mr. Prettyman arrived in the course of a few minutes, and making a low bow, took from off his shoulder a large bag full of the much-needed articles. He begged to inform the ladies that the young gentlemen had mentioned as how a party down on the beach had had the sad misfortune of having every bit of shoe leather carried out to sea, and had desired him to bring some boots to fit on. He had made it his business to select the very best from his stock, and was proud and happy to wait on such gentry.

Miss Campbell thanked him for attending so promptly to the order.

The children were much amused when the boots were produced and handed round, the make of them being something rather different to those they were in the habit of wearing.

"Oh!" exclaimed Maud, as a heavy pair was given her to try on, "these are something like boots: plenty of good large nails, and leather laces, too. I hope they will fit." Being a full size for her, she found no difficulty in getting them on. She was bent on keeping them, if possible; so, drawing the laces together as tightly as she could, stood up in great glee to show her aunt what a beautiful fit they were. "I could," she said, "walk miles in these, and never feel tired. Aunt Milicent, may I have them?"

"Yes," replied Miss Campbell, "provided you do not wear them in the house when we go home, or I shall be thinking we have some little ploughboy with us."

Maud was quite content with this, and delighted at her possession of the much-admired boots. Fortunately every one found a pair they could wear, and Mr. Prettyman was well pleased with the sale of his goods. It was, he remarked, a bad job for the gentlefolks losing their things, but good for trade. He had sold as much shoe leather that day as would take him a month to dispose of without such an accident had taken place; and thanking the ladies for their custom, took his departure.

By degrees the party began to disperse. Maud walked on by herself, every now and then looking round to see if Harold was following; but he seemed more disposed to remain with Frank Willoughby, who was giving him an account of his life at school.

"I shall," said Frank, "have to work tremendously hard for the next three months to get ready for the examination. I'm almost sorry to leave Dr. Montgomery's, for it's awfully jolly there, especially during summer, for then the boys go out boating very often. Of course we have to stick to our work, and get through a certain amount in the day, but when that's done we have our fling. I don't think you would find it a bad speculation if you could persuade your father to let you go there, and I think you told me you would shortly be leaving your present school."

"Yes," replied Harold, "after the midsummer term. I should like to go back with you very much."

"Just remember one thing, my good fellow," remarked Frank, "we should not be long together, but I could put you up to a few dodges before I left; besides, if a fellow is plucky, he soon fights his own way. You must stand your ground from the first, and let the boys see you won't put up with any humbug. But, I say, just look, Harold, isn't that Maud Hamilton waving her handkerchief? I expect there's something wrong; let's make haste and go to the rescue." The boys ran to where Maud was standing, looking very much put out.

"Is this the way you keep an appointment, Harold?" she asked. "Here I've been waiting I don't know how long, whilst you and Frank are talking as if there was nothing to be done; it's such a pity when everything is ready. See what I have managed to bring away." And Maud showed him part of a roast fowl, some bread, and a number of tarts, which she had carefully tied up in a cloth. "Now," she said, "haven't I secured a good store?"

"You have, indeed," he replied; "and I don't see why we should not go on our expedition at once. I daresay Frank will come with us, which will make it all the pleasanter."

"All right," said Frank; "but where are we to get a boat?"

They decided to walk on some distance, where they saw one lying on the beach, not far from a small black shed, which they concluded must belong to the owner. Maud, at the prospect of going with the boys, had quite recovered her temper, and chatted away, much to their amusement, until they reached the shed, at the door of which sat an old man, smoking his pipe, and enjoying the sun.

"Good afternoon, young gentlemen," he said; "can I do anything for you?"

"That you can," replied Frank, "if the boat yonder is yours. We want to hire one for a few hours."

Old Ben, (for that was the sailor's name,) inquired who was going with them, for if they were alone he would not take the responsibility of letting them have it.

"Oh, as to *that*," answered Frank, "you need not fear; boating is nothing new to me; seldom a day passes that I am not on the water. Very soon I hope to go to sea altogether."

"Maybe you will, sir," replied Ben, "but depend on't, there'll be older heads than yours when you are there. It isn't altogether I'm so much afeard about your not knowing how to handle an oar; but it's coming on nasty squally weather, and these parts of the coast are treacherous when that's the case. You mustn't think of taking the young lady with you; surely you wouldn't expose *her* to no dangers."

"I'm not the least afraid," interposed Maud. "I'm so fond of the sea, and have come a long distance on purpose to go fishing."

"I can't help it, missie; but my boat don't stir from this yer landing-place to-day with *my* consent and knowledge: it's not fit weather."

"Not fit!" exclaimed Harold; "why, it's a beautiful day, just the weather for a row."

"I know my business best," said Ben; "the weather may be all right for land folks, but it isn't for the sea."

Frank burst into a laugh of disbelief, saying, "Why, there isn't the least sign of a storm anywhere. You only say that to frighten us."

"My eyes," replied the old man, "see signs where yours don't; and you won't have no boat of mine if you offers me gold for it. It shall never be said that Ben Ward was the cause of your coming to harm by the letting out of his boat for any money he could make."

"Do! please do!" pleaded Maud. "You will spoil everything if you won't let us have it."

"No, missie; I've told you I won't, and I

won't. I'm downright sorry to disappoint you; but there's an end of it."

Maud's indignation knew no bounds, to think they could not be trusted by themselves, and on such a beautiful day as it was, too. What did it matter if there were a few dark clouds? they would soon lift. And she shook her head, muttering her displeasure at the way they were treated.

"Now, young gentlemen, it's no mortal use your waiting here; you'd better take the little 'un back to her friends." And having given this advice, Ben Ward put the pipe again into his mouth, locked the shed, and well securing his boat, walked himself off.

As he left the beach, the children stood in a state of vexation and disappointment. Harold's pride made him writhe, to think he should be considered incapable of managing a boat, whilst Maud declared Ben was the most horrid old man she had ever come across. Frank Willoughby, however, tried to persuade his companions that, tiresome as it was, perhaps after all it would be wisest not to venture on the sea that afternoon, but wait another opportunity, when, too, there would be more time; "for," he remarked, "it must be past three o'clock, and at seven Miss Campbell said they were to start."

"Do as you choose," replied Harold; "I intend getting a boat if possible, and am not to be so easily frightened by what that old muff has said. Make up your mind, for I am going on further, where I see several boats, and no doubt shall be able to hire one without much difficulty."

Frank hesitated; he would have enjoyed the expedition, and to be considered as wanting in courage was very trying; but still, after all Ben Ward's warnings, it would be wrong to go. So he told Harold he had quite decided to remain on shore. "And," he added, "don't be vexed if I beg you *not* to take Maud. If any harm should happen to her you would be so miserable to think you had acted in opposition to all that had been advised."

"Thank you for your sage advice," replied Harold; "but I'm not in the humour to listen to a sermon, so shut up, my good fellow. I'm too much of a sailor to keep on land on account of a few dark clouds."

CHAPTER VI.

Self-Will and its Consequences.

During the discussion between the two boys, Maud felt very uncomfortable. She knew Frank was right, but her great desire to go fishing overcame all scruples. When their conversation came to an end she asked Harold what he had decided on.

"Decided on?" he repeated. "Why, to shove off in the first boat I can get hold of. You'd better return with Frank, who is frightened at the idea of a little rough water. If it's not fit for him to go, it certainly can't be for a girl."

"Oh, do please let me go," pleaded Maud; "just try me; I am sure I can make myself useful by steering the boat."

Harold did not like refusing the little girl's earnest request, so consented to her accompanying him. Maud walked off by his side, full of life and spirits, carrying as best she could the fishing rod and a basket filled with provisions. Frank stood watching them. He ventured more than once to call to Maud, and beg her to return; but she only laughed, saying she meant to enjoy herself whilst she could.

It took the two children much longer than they supposed it would to reach the spot they intended. At last they came up to a number of sailors, who were standing together, loitering away an idle hour talking of a sail they hoped to take that night, one of them remarking, he feared if the weather turned out as stormy as it seemed to promise, they would not have much luck. The men looked with some curiosity at the two children as they approached; for the little village of Seaforth was a quiet, old-fashioned place, only now and then enlivened by visitors, who came for a day's pleasure to enjoy the beautiful scenery by which it was surrounded. Harold walked straight up to the men, and was on the point of saying what he wanted, when to his disappointment they walked off.

"What a set of savages the people are in this place," he exclaimed, in a passion. "I only wish Frank hadn't been such a stupid, and come with us, then I wouldn't stop another minute, but make use of a boat without asking any one's leave."

These words were hardly said when he was somewhat startled by a man suddenly appearing from behind one of the cliffs close by. Walking up to the children, he touched his hat, saying, "Beg pardon, sir, but are you wanting to go on the water?"

"Yes, that I do," was the eager reply. "Can you manage it for us?"

"I can manage it well enough," answered the man, "if you make it worth my while to do so. The boat ain't altogether mine; it partly belongs to my father, who you were talking to down yonder by the shed. He's a crusty old chap, and won't let no one have it when he's stubborn like, and what's more, would prevent my making a bit of money when I have the chance, which ain't often."

Harold offered three shillings if he could have the boat at once for a couple of hours. The offer was a tempting one to the young man. He knew how acceptable the money would be for his wife and children, and although he had his misgivings as to the wisdom of allowing Harold to hire the boat, the thoughts of the hungry mouths at home waiting to be filled overcame his better judgment, and it ended by his saying, "Come along, sir, follow me, and I'll accommodate you. We must walk back again to the shed, and just mind we keep clear of the old man."

On their reaching the spot, Ben Ward was nowhere in sight, so his son, not caring that he had expressly refused the boat being used, loosened it from its fastenings and shoved it afloat. He insisted, however, on going with the children.

"Can't we have a sail?" suggested Harold. "There seems quite enough wind to fill it, and it will be easier work than rowing."

"Oh, yes, I can readily manage that," was Jack Ward's confident answer. And the sail was immediately set.

The boat went briskly before the wind, and much talking and laughing prevailed. Jack was no restraint on their amusement: indeed, he added to it in no small degree by relating his adventures, and the sights he had seen during his seafaring life. Maud thoroughly enjoyed it; it was much pleasanter than she expected skimming the water so quickly and quietly.

"Isn't it a pity," she remarked, " Frank wouldn't join us? I didn't think he would go off like he did; he seemed up to any amount of fun. Well, when he hears how we've succeeded, he will act differently another time, I fancy. When shall we begin to fish?"

"I think," replied Harold, " if we could take the boat round that large rock that juts out some distance into the sea, the water would be beautifully deep, and smoother than it is here;

it appears to me the very spot to select for such a purpose. What do you say?". he asked Jack Ward.

"It ain't very easy to steer a boat round them nasty sharp points, as one's apt to come against 'em; but if you try and keep clear of 'em, I'll do my best," replied the man.

As it was, the wind, blowing steadily from the land, had carried them much further than they reckoned.

"All right," said Harold, "I'll be careful enough." And after a while they reached the place decided on.

Much to their delight, they found they could climb up the rock, which in several places overhung the sea, Jack Ward being quite content to remain meanwhile in the boat, and indulge in a smoke.

"Oh, how beautiful!" exclaimed Maud; "I am sure I shall not wish to go home in a hurry. I wouldn't have missed this expedition on any account."

"Now then," said Harold, "as you are safe and happy, I think, before we settle down, I shall get into the boat, and go with Jack, and see what it looks like round that other point. You remain where you are."

Maud did not much like being left alone, and

began to wonder what she should do if a shark were to appear; but she thought it best to keep these dreadful thoughts to herself, or Harold would no longer consider her the brave girl he evidently did at present; so, endeavouring to hide her alarm, she only remarked it seemed a pity not to be satisfied with the nice place they had already found, without going in search of another. Harold, however, was not inclined to give up the little trip, and much to her dismay shoved off in the boat, leaving her in an anxious state of mind. For at least a quarter of an hour Maud sat alone, her thoughts occupied with all kinds of imaginable evils, when at last, to her relief, she heard the splashing of oars, and in a few minutes the boat appeared, with Harold in high spirits.

"Here I am," he cried; "it's just as well I went, for I've discovered a jolly place: this is nothing compared to it. You must get down again, and jump into the boat as well as you can. Mind you don't miss your footing, or you will have an awful ducking in the water, and I don't promise I can pull you out again."

It was rather difficult for the little girl to manage the descent, the rock being sharp and steep. Harold was unable to give her much assistance, and Jack Ward had his part to do in seeing the boat did not move away when Maud would be giving a spring to reach it.

"Oh my, it is so hard to do," she said, looking very frightened; "I don't think I can jump so far down all by myself."

"That's nonsense," replied Harold; "you told me only an hour ago you would not be afraid of any dangers, and I'm sure this is a precious little one; pray be quick, or we shall be all night before we are settled."

Seeing he was becoming impatient, Maud in trepidation made a leap, fortunately succeeding in the attempt, and was most thankful to find herself once again in the boat.

Jack Ward, with some good strokes of the oars, soon reached a creek where he said he could manage to get the boat sufficiently close to the rock to admit of their landing. Having done this, he secured it with a rope, and then they clambered up to the top. The view was certainly very beautiful from the height on which they stood, and the children were charmed. They did not notice some heavy clouds that were gathering, but, pleased with their present pleasure, did not care to think of anything that might destroy it. Maud was perfectly satisfied with the arrangements, and watched with great interest Harold's preparations for fishing.

When at last the line was thrown in, they sat waiting for the bait to take, and amused themselves with chatting. Maud enjoyed the description Harold gave of his school experiences, and very wonderful he appeared in her eyes at all the marvellous things he had done, the narrow escapes he had had, both on land and sea; and heartily she laughed when he recounted the wars that sometimes took place with the boys in bolstering matches. He likewise gave a graphic account of a grand supper they had one night in the dormitory.

"Having waited," he said, "for an opportunity when we thought the head master would be away from home, we purchased a tempting collection in the way of lobsters, gingerbreads, tarts, and apples, not to mention numerous kinds of sweets. These were carefully concealed between boxes; and the bottles of ginger beer, being thrust amongst the feathers in the pillows, were considered in perfect security."

When Harold reached this exciting point in his description, Maud felt compelled to exclaim at the clever arrangements, saying she would certainly have some idea now how to manage when her time came for going to school; she had never heard anything so capital. "But I am interrupting you; pray go on, I am longing to hear how the supper went off."

"Well," continued Harold, "the night we fixed on came in good time. It had taken us nearly a week to get the things, as we could only manage it by degrees, so as to avoid suspicion. We went as usual to the dormitory at nine, most of us getting into bed without taking off more than our jackets and boots, and there we remained, keeping perfectly quiet until it would be safe to commence our repast. By half-past ten, Gilbert, the eldest of our number, gave the word of command for all to turn out of bed, which we accordingly did, and began arranging the food. Gilbert's bed was to be used as a table, and I can tell you there was a first-rate spread. After tucking in for some time, Topples, a little chap, was told to go round the room, and collect the mugs we used for our teeth, as these were to do duty as glasses for drinking the ginger beer out of. The little stupid went right enough to get them, but in coming back across the room never noticed we had placed some of the bottles on the floor, and went tumbling over them, dropping the mugs in his fright, and smashing the

bottles to pieces. I shall never forget that
night as long as I live. The noise was something tremendous, and all the more so from the
extreme quietness of the house. Frightened as
we were, we could not help laughing at the
sight of Tommy Topples rolling amongst the
broken bottles, whilst streams of frothy ginger
beer ran in all directions over the floor. However, it did not do to remain as we were, and
each boy made for his bed, excepting Gilbert,
who knew he could find no resting-place in his,
considering how it was covered with the eatables, so he took refuge in mine. We soon
heard some one coming up the stairs, and in
another minute the door was thrown open by
no less a person than the head master himself,
(for he had not gone from home as we reckoned
on.) You might have heard a pin drop, we
were so quiet. I peeped from under the counterpane to see what he looked like, and the
expression of his face told only too plainly what
we might expect. We had, as a precaution,
only turned on the gas very slightly, but old
Sinclair put it on to the full, and took a survey
of the whole room. What a frightful state it
was in. We had demolished three lobsters,
the shells of which were scattered in all directions; jam tarts partly eaten, and hurriedly

thrown down by the frightened boys, added to the confusion of the scene. As to Tommy Topples, the shock had evidently deprived him of the use of his legs, otherwise he would no doubt have made an attempt to conceal himself under his bedclothes; as it was, the poor fellow lay exactly where he fell, with his eyes fixed on his master, waiting to see what sentence would be pronounced by him. It was not long before we knew our fate; the following morning, when the boys assembled for study, the culprits were each called up by name to Sinclair's desk. There we stood, nine of us, all in a row. Having spoken of our conduct in pretty strong terms of condemnation, we received a severe caning, only a difference being made in Tommy Topples' case, for, being so much younger than us, he was not considered equally guilty. This was the last supper we had, for we did not think it answered well; and I advise you, Maud, although you would not have the same punishment to fear, to be careful, and consider the possible consequences before you have an entertainment when you go to school."

"Yes," she replied; "the beginning of the story is very interesting to listen to, but the ending makes one think twice."

The time had passed without either of them remembering how late it was getting.

"Shall we see if we have caught any fish?" asked Maud.

The line was drawn up, but no victim appeared on the hook.

Harold laughed, saying, "It's well we haven't to depend on food from the fruits of our labour. But, dear me, just look to the right; I'm afraid the old sailor's words are coming true, and we shall have a storm."

Even whilst he was speaking some heavy drops of rain began to fall.

"I declare I'm quite cold," said Maud. "Here, Trusty, come here, sir." (And the dog went up to his mistress.) "You nice old dog, lie down and make my feet warm." And she placed them on Trusty's warm coat.

Harold was feeling very uneasy, but did not like to say anything more to his companion. Telling her to remain where she was with the dog, he said he would go and see what had become of Jack Ward. The man had sauntered some distance from where the children had settled themselves, and after awhile made himself comfortable, finally falling asleep. It took Harold some considerable time before he came upon him, and when he did so, he quickly roused the sailor.

"Jack, Jack," he said, pulling the man by the arm, "wake up; it's time we were going back."

"All right, sir," replied Ward, as he stood up and stretched himself; "it strikes me there ain't no time to lose, for see, its getting terrible squally."

The sun, they observed, was near setting, and big black clouds hid it from view. The wind, too, which had been but a slight breeze when they started, had greatly increased, and there seemed every probability that the storm Ben Ward had foretold would be upon them before very long.

Just then a clap of thunder made Harold start; he thought of Maud, left alone as she was; he knew how frightened she would be, and begged the sailor to make as much haste as possible, and return to the poor child.

They found Maud crying bitterly. "Oh, Harold," she exclaimed, on seeing him, "I thought something had happened, you have been away such a long time. Isn't this storm dreadful? I'm nearly wet through, it rains so fast. Do take us back again, Jack," she said, appealingly, to the man.

"Ay, ay, missy," he answered, cheerily; "don't you be afeard; we will be home again in a jiffy."

But the going home again was not so easy a thing as they imagined. It was with the greatest effort Maud and Harold managed to get down the rock and into the boat, and they soon found that going against the wind was a very different thing from going with it. The boat began to toss about in a way that was anything but pleasant, especially to Maud, and Jack Ward had great difficulty in managing the sail, till the boat lay over alarmingly on one side; so with infinite trouble he took down the sail, and again had recourse to the oars. They got on a little better now, Harold making himself of use, as far as his strength would admit, in helping to row. All poor Maud could do was to lie at the bottom of the boat, with her face buried in her dog's rough coat, and wish she had never come. How often it is the case that when children think they know better than their elders, they get into trouble.

There was no other boat out; wiser heads than theirs had seen the storm coming, and had safely secured them in the little cove of Seaforth. So Maud and Harold were alone with only Jack Ward, an angry sky above them, and still angrier sea around them, whilst the wind was every minute growing louder and louder, lashing the waves into greater fury.

Jack and Harold rowed with all their strength. The tide was running very strong, and the sailor knew that they were drifting far higher up than Seaforth; but could they only reach the shore anywhere, all would be well.

CHAPTER VII.

In the Storm; or, Life and Death.

After watching his companions almost out of sight, Frank walked back, intending to join the others. He felt very uncomfortable, for he had but little doubt that notwithstanding all Ben Ward had said, Harold would if possible persuade some other fisherman to let him hire his boat; and that it was not safe nor fitting they should go was quite certain. He quite resolved to tell Mrs. Graham and Miss Campbell exactly what had taken place, not omitting the conversation they had had with the old sailor who had foretold the storm, and which Frank saw was already brewing up.

He was much disappointed, on reaching that part of the beach where he expected to find them, to see no vestige of a single creature. "Perhaps," he said to himself, "they found it cold as the sun went down, and have gone inland to seek some place to have their tea. I should be glad of some, too, for I'm anything but warm. I only wish Harold and Maud had not been so foolish, but had come back with me. As it is, I must be sharp, and try to find out what has become of the others, which will not be so very difficult in such a small village."

No one being about, Frank knocked at one of the cottage doors, which was opened by a fisherman, who, in reply to the inquiries he made, said he had observed a party pass by half an hour since. He could not be sure, but he fancied they took the direct road to the village; anyhow, he was certain they were not on the beach. "Very likely, sir, you would find them put up at the 'Red House,' and if you are a stranger in these parts, and would like me to show you the way, I'll do so with pleasure."

Frank gladly accepted the offer, asking the man, as they walked along, what he thought of the weather.

"There can't be two minds about it, sir; bad, very bad. It's to be hoped there are no boats far out just now, or there's little chance for them who are on the sea of ever reaching the shore again. I reckon before another hour has passed over our heads we shall have as big a storm as have visited these parts for a long time; and if I ain't mistaken, I feels heavy drops a falling already."

It was quite true, for within a few minutes the rain began to descend in good earnest.

Frank's anxious face attracted the sailor's notice. "I hope, young gentleman," he asked, "you've no cause for anxiety; I mean that there's no one belonging to you on the water?"

"I am sorry to say," replied Frank, "that two of our party went off not very long ago."

"Bless me," said the man, "that's a bad job, and a downright shame for any one to push a boat off on such a day as this; they ought to have known better, with the weather threatening as it have been all the afternoon. But cheer up, sir; perhaps a seeing the heavy clouds gathering, they've turned back, and are safe enough on shore."

They had trudged on some distance, talking in this way, when the man, pointing to the farther end of a long straggling street, observed, "There's the 'Red House,' sir, and a fine place it is; it's frequented by a good many of the gentry as comes here for a day's pleasuring in the summer time. Sally Megs, who keeps it, is a rare one for knowing how to turn a penny, and I don't blame her neither, for she's a lone body, and ever since her old man took bad and died, has had no one but herself to look to for a livelihood."

We must leave Frank Willoughby and the sailor for a while, making their way to Sally Megs, and rejoin Miss Campbell and her party, whom we left on the beach.

As the evening came on, they began to find it too cold to remain any longer near the water, and decided on trying to find some place where they might take their tea comfortably. They were soon attracted by the large board hanging over the door of Sally Megs' house, which proclaimed, in letters of bold character, that there was "good accommodation for man and beast," also, "Tea made on the shortest notice possible."

"The very thing we want," said Miss Campbell, reading the notice. "No doubt everything will be in primitive style; that, however, is a secondary consideration, if we can only succeed in getting a sufficient supply of eatables, for I think every one looks quite ready for a substantial meal. I hope those three other children will soon join us," she remarked to Mrs. Graham; "they have been away long enough, and Maud will be overtiring herself, I'm afraid."

"No doubt," replied Mrs. Graham, "when

they miss us off the beach, they will come in search."

Desiring the children to wait outside, the two ladies entered the "Red House." A bright rosy-faced-looking little woman came forward, and making a deep bow, inquired what it might be her pleasing duty to do for the ladies, at the same time throwing open the door of a large room, the floor of which was well covered with sand. Miss Campbell soon made her wishes known, whilst Sally Megs stood receiving the orders given with evident satisfaction, for there seemed to her a hope of making some good profits with so many hungry mouths to be filled.

The children were delighted with the old-fashioned place, and asked if they might have the fire lighted; it would make it so nice and warm, they said. So Peggy, the little maid-of-all-work, was sent in to do as they wished, and in a short time a bright blazing fire burned in the grate.

Sally Megs meanwhile bustled in and out, first with a curious collection of cups and saucers, which must from all appearances have been in the Megs family many years; these were followed by plates of cake, the quality of which was doubtful. As to bread and butter, in Sally's eyes it was the staff of life; if one might judge so by the quantity she supplied her guests with. Having arranged everything to her satisfaction, she informed the ladies tea was ready, and hoped they would make themselves comfortable.

They had been seated for some time, doing ample justice to the food provided by the thoughtful Sally, talking and laughing merrily over the morning's adventures, when Miss Campbell exclaimed, "Dear me, did you notice those vivid flashes of lightning? And now it is beginning to rain. Where can those children be?"

She rose and went to the window. In every direction the clouds looked dark and wild: evidently a tremendous storm was not far off.

"I shall go and look for them; Maud will be wet through, and, I fear, quite ill, exposed to such dreadful weather. Mrs. Graham, you remain here with the children whilst nurse comes with me. If we are detained, pray do not wait, but return home, and I will follow as soon as I can."

Having made this arrangement, and wrapping herself in a waterproof cloak, she went out with nurse to face the storm. They hurried along, every minute adding to the anxiety they felt. It was but a short distance they had walked, when they saw Frank coming towards them, with the sailor. Miss Campbell felt a sad misgiving when she perceived Harold and Maud were not with them.

When Frank caught sight of Miss Campbell, he ran up to her, exclaiming, "Oh, Miss Campbell, Maud and Harold are out in a boat in all this storm, and there is but little chance of their ever getting back again; isn't it dreadful? They would go; I begged them not to, but Harold thought I was a coward, and frightened without reason, so he left me, taking Maud with him, and when I saw he was quite determined, I returned to tell you what had happened."

And Frank paused for breath, which his rapid talking and the wind together had almost taken away.

Miss Campbell stood, with her hands tightly clasped together, listening to the news Frank was giving her; she felt terribly anxious. She tried, as she always did, to carry her troubles to the only Source of comfort; but her nerves were much shaken by the suddenness of the tidings, and she could not help fearing the worst.

"We must hasten without delay," she said, "and find out if they have returned; even now they may be in one of the cottages drying their clothes. I think," she added, addressing the sailor who had joined them, "if you will, it would be best for you to come with us; you may rely on my making it worth your while to do so."

"I shall be only too glad to be of any service," he replied. "I've been born and bred to the sea, and don't feel at home out of the reach of salt water. We must hope for the best; God grant the young lady and gentleman may be out of danger and safely ashore: but if not, there are those who wouldn't stand by idle, and not stretch out a helping hand to save a fellow-creature. It's rough weather for the likes of you, ma'am, to be out; but I suppose you wouldn't find no rest if you was to stop indoors."

"No, my good man, you say truly; I could not know rest or peace whilst we are in uncertainty as to the fate of those poor children."

It took them quite half an hour to reach the spot which Frank pointed out as the place they started from. The beach was entirely deserted; the men who before had been strolling about had now disappeared, having drawn up their boats, and secured them from being damaged by the sea.

Miss Campbell shuddered as she stood watching the dark raging water, the waves rising to an immense height, and then dashing with fury against the cliffs.

"I'll go and call some of my comrades to come down and see what can be done," said the sailor. And in the course of another ten minutes several of the men had assembled on the beach.

Ben Ward was amongst the number, and to his dismay and annoyance he soon discovered that his boat had disappeared.

"Why, Ward," said one old man, "your Jack took her out nigh an hour ago; I seed him shove off myself, and was summut surprised at your letting him go out such weather, as every one could see we was a going to have a storm; but it was none of my business."

"They'll never live in yonder sea," remarked another man, as he gazed out on the angry waters. And indeed there seemed but small chance of it.

Old Ben endeavoured to do his best to console Miss Campbell, telling her to keep up; perhaps the little 'uns had reached the shore before the storm had got so high. "The poor bairns," he said; "we must do all we can for them, and leave the rest to the Almighty."

"Yes," she answered, gently, whilst the tears streamed down her pale cheeks; "the great sea has them at its mercy, but there is One who sees them, even in the midst of the storm and tempest, who holds the waters in the hollow of His hand." And as she spoke she prayed that God would bring them safe home again.

"If I reckon rightly," continued Ben, "from what I know of the young gentleman, he's not one to give in easy when trouble and danger is at hand: so depend upon it, whatever he may have to go through himself, he'll look sharp enough after the little girl. I was a sitting by the boat shed when the two came along this afternoon, and I thought to myself at the time that the young gent was meant to ride the sea, he seemed reg'lar cut out for it. As to the lassie, a prettier one the sun never shined upon, it's my belief, and when I refused to let them have the boat, how she shook her head, a throwing them thick curls of her's about, quite indignant like to think I would not trust them. I never knew until now how it ended, for I went back to my missus, who was waiting for me down home."

He was interrupted from saying more by one of the men calling to him to look at some dark object on the water. Ben immediately mounted to the top of one of the cliffs, with his glass in his hand, and through it he thought he could make out in the far distance a boat struggling with the waves, but he could not be quite certain.

The nearest life-boat was seven miles off, so there was no chance of obtaining that. However, Ben Ward determined to do what he could, and going back to the beach, began to draw one of the boats to the water's edge.

"What are you going to do?" asked Patterson, the old weather-beaten sailor who had spoken first.

"I am going after those who are in peril," he said, with a stern look on his face.

"It's a foolhardy business, your venturing on the sea in a storm like this; as it is, I fear it's all over with them poor things. But if you are willing to risk your life, you shan't go single-handed; mine is worth nothing to nobody but to my old woman," he added, with a choking voice.

"No, Patterson," said Ben Ward, firmly,

"I'll not take you. It's not my Jack I think about so much as those others; he can swim, and has a chance, but the two children will be very helpless in a sea like this."

"I'll go with you, Ward," exclaimed a strong young fellow, coming forward.

"That's right, Festing," was Ward's answer. And he grasped the young man's hand with a hearty shake. "By God's help you and I will save them."

They got into the boat without further delay, with ropes and life-belts, and anything else they could think of, the men on the shore watching them with intense interest, and wishing them God speed.

Miss Campbell sank down, no longer able to control her emotion, which made even the rough sailors declare they had in their time come across a deal of trouble; but to see the poor lady in that 'ere state was more than they knew how to stand. Frank, too, was crying bitterly as he thought of his friends losing their lives in so dreadful a manner.

At last one of the men broke the silence, saying, "It's a sad ending for such young 'uns as they be; but there's no help for them now, it's my belief. I wish we could persuade the good lady to go back to the village, and get under shelter; it's no earthly use her keeping out in this weather, a beating the very life out of her. You try and see what you can do," he said to old Patterson.

But nothing would induce Miss Campbell to comply with their request; she refused to leave the beach until she could hear something of those missing.

Finding it useless to say more, the fishermen continued to walk on, and at Miss Campbell's request promised to climb to the highest part of the cliff, and watch their comrades as they made their way over the rough sea, whilst she and Frank had to content themselves to wait where they were; but the waiting and suspense were very hard to bear.

In the course of half an hour the men returned; they had nothing encouraging to relate, and indeed there seemed very little hope that either of the boats could live through the storm.

And now it was useless to remain longer, for the wind had increased in height, and the air was very cold. There was nothing to be seen but the white foam of the waves as they dashed against the cliffs, and soon it would be dark; so, though Miss Campbell would fain have stayed, she felt it would be best and wisest to return to the "Red House."

On reaching Sally Megs' abode, they found Mrs. Graham and the children still there; indeed, it was not likely they would leave for Riversdale until they had received some tidings of the missing ones. Little Ethel had gone to bed, and had forgotten her troubles in sleep, but the others crowded round Miss Campbell with eager, anxious faces, to hear what she had to say. There was not much to be told, but what there was only added to the terrible fears they felt before.

"We can do nothing to help our darlings," said Miss Campbell, in a voice she vainly tried to make steady; "we must leave them in God's hands. And now, my dear children, I think you must all try and take some rest; you may rely on our letting you know directly we hear anything of Harold and Maud."

Poor Edith and Wilfrid! It was difficult for them to do as they were directed, but seeing the distress of Mrs. Graham and Miss Campbell, they went with the others to the rooms prepared for them. Not, however, before they knelt down, and prayed earnestly and fervently for the safety of those in peril, did they seek the repose they so much needed.

At last, towards midnight, there came tidings. The young man, Bill Festing, who had so generously volunteered to go with Ward, arrived with the joyful news that both the children were safe, but too exhausted to be moved yet.

The two ladies lost no time in accompanying the sailor, hurrying with all the speed possible to Ben Ward's cottage, where Harold and Maud had been taken. A respectable, elderly woman opened the door, placing her finger on her lips to warn them that there was necessity for silence.

She beckoned them in, and having carefully shut the door, told them in a whisper not to be alarmed; the young gentleman and lady were safe, and in a beautiful sleep, in an inner room to which she pointed. "But," she added, "it will ease your minds to see them, and you can do so without disturbing them, I fancy, by going in gently."

Very quietly, but trembling with agitation, the ladies entered the little room. On a small bed, which was exquisitely clean, lay Harold, in a deep slumber; he looked pale, otherwise no one would have imagined he had gone through any perils.

Maud was lying on an old sofa in a tiny

room above; she seemed feverish and restless; every now and then half broken sentences escaped her lips. She would speak of the dark water, begging Harold to hold her tightly, or she would slip off the boat and be lost. These and similar exclamations showed plainly that the child's mind was wandering on the one subject.

As Miss Campbell sat by her side, and gazed at the fair and lovely face, with the golden hair clustering round her head in rich abundance, and she thought of how she had been nearly snatched away by death, she pressed a loving kiss on her forehead, whilst a prayer of gratitude went up to heaven for the great mercy vouchsafed.

After a while Maud sank into a calm, quiet sleep, much to Miss Campbell's relief, for she could not help feeling anxious whilst she tossed about in such a disturbed manner. The child, she knew, was not strong, though well and healthy in a general way, and it made her fear that a sudden shock and exposure, such as she had gone through, might prove serious to her.

The following morning set in with all the brightness of a summer's day. The storm had entirely passed away, and the sea looked smooth and pleasant, as if it had never held anything so precious in its bosom, and played with it as a thing of nought.

Both children appeared themselves again, with the exception perhaps of looking rather paler than usual. They begged to be allowed to go to the "Red House" for breakfast, and surprise all those who were waiting there.

Miss Campbell did not trust herself to say much to old Ward and Bill Festing just then; she merely shook hands with the noble sailors who had risked their own lives to save those belonging to her.

"God alone," she said, "can reward you as you deserve. When I am more myself again I shall be better able to express what I feel, and trust it may be in my power to render you both some service which may prove of real benefit to you."

They begged her not to say anything; they had only done what was the plain duty of any man, and were but too thankful that they had, with God's help, been able to rescue the children.

It is needless to describe the rejoicing when the meeting took place at the "Red House." Maud was the first to make her way into the room where nurse and the others were assem-

IN THE STORM.   109

bled. Her arms were soon round Edith's neck, and the sisters wept for joy. "Safe! safe!" seemed the one word they liked to hear best.

And could it be wondered at? for had not Maud seen death staring her in the face? And such a death, too! Had she not seen Harold dashed down into the waters, and lost in the darkness, whilst she herself only seemed left for a few minutes before apparently sharing the same fate? They were not interrupted by those around them, for it was easy to understand what the two little girls must be feeling.

Before the party left Seaforth, old Ben Ward, by Miss Campbell's request, came up to give an account of all he knew of the sad event. His tale was listened to with breathless interest.

It appeared, from what he said, that Jack Ward and Harold had gone on rowing, and trying their best to pull the boat towards the shore, so long as their strength held out; but the waves dashed over them, and there was danger every minute that the boat would fill and sink.

At last they were forced to give up, and let the boat drift whither it would at the mercy of the wind and waves. For some time it rode safely on the top of one wave, and down in the hollow of another; but at last, one stronger than the rest dashed against and overturned it, and they were plunged into the water.

At first they managed to keep hold of the boat, but the darkness of night was rapidly coming on, and there was no light anywhere near them; their hands, too, became numbed with the coldness of the water, and Jack Ward declared he should make for the shore. He was a good swimmer, and it was the only chance they would have of being saved, if he could reach the land, and send some one to help them.

In vain Harold, in an agony of despair, implored him not to leave them, whilst poor little Maud, almost dead with terror, clung to the young man. But Jack Ward's mind was made up, and bidding the weeping child hold on fast to the boat, without another word swam off, and was soon lost in the darkness. And so the two poor children were left alone, waiting in helpless despair for the death which was to all appearances so surely coming upon them.

Harold clung with desperate energy to the

IN THE STORM.

boat, but Maud became unconscious, and gradually relaxed her hold, and had it not been for the faithful dog, who had accompanied them, and who, with all the sagacity of his noble race, seized his little mistress by her dress, she would have drifted away. But help came, and only just in time; a few minutes longer, and it would have been too late.

Harold had quite given up all hope, when he heard some one calling out, "Boat ahoy! boat ahoy!" Quickly he answered it with an eager "Here, here." Poor boy! his voice was rather faint, but, thank God, the men heard him, and as far as their eyes, accustomed to the darkness, could judge, they must be close to a rock which they knew was quite near.

In another few minutes both children were safely in the fisherman's boat, "Trusty" still watching over Maud, as if afraid she might be swept away by the waves.

It required all the strength the men had to pull their boat to shore; but when once they were safe on land, they quickly carried the exhausted children to Ward's cottage, where they received every attention necessary under the circumstances.

Such was the substance of the story that Ben Ward told to the eager listening ears, and deep thankfulness arose in their hearts that He, at whose word the stormy wind ariseth, which lifteth up the waves thereof, had listened to them when they had cried unto Him in their trouble, and had delivered those so dear to them out of their distress. Yes; they had much to thank God for, and Miss Campbell could not refrain from weeping silently for a few minutes, as the old sailor, in his quaint but intelligent manner, had given the account of all that had transpired.

Having arranged that Ben Ward and Bill Festing should go to Riversdale in the course of the week, and being anxious to return home as soon as possible, Miss Campbell, with the others, left Seaforth by the eleven a.m. train.

Sally Megs was quite sorry to part with them, saying she had not known her house so lively for many a long day, and hoped they would come that way again.

As to Jack Ward, suffice it to say that after leaving the two children to their fate, it was with difficulty he managed to swim to shore, and when at last he stole into one of the boat sheds, and laid himself down, exhausted from his exertions, his mind was too uneasy to allow him to sleep. He knew that he was guilty of a mean, cowardly act, and for many a day he skulked about, thoroughly ashamed of himself.

When his father upbraided him by saying, "You took them, and you left them, and it's a miracle they ever came back alive," his only answer was, "I wasn't going to bide there to be drowned, so I did the best I could for myself. And after all," he added, with a half scornful laugh, "I daresay we weren't in half the danger we thought ourselves; and if they had been drowned it would not have been my fault, for the young gent was bent on going somehow, and if I had not taken him, he'd a gone by hisself with the little girl."

It was many days before the excitement consequent on the past events allowed the children to settle down. Miss Campbell was only too thankful to see Maud had not suffered seriously, and thought entire relaxation from study would be beneficial.

Maud declared she would never leave her sister again for any expedition, however delightful; and as to a desert island, much as she longed to spend her life on one, all idea of such happiness would be entirely given up unless Edith were to be with her.

To Nurse Grey all that had happened had been a great shock, and the poor old soul seemed unable to rest, neither could she bear Maud out of her sight, but watched her about from place to place, saying, if anything had happened to the sweet lamb she should never have held up her head again.

CHAPTER VIII.

Off to School.

The winter, with its sharp frosts and cold biting winds, had passed away, and with it had gone all the dreariness of that cheerless season. The trees were budding forth their fresh young leaves, showing that summer was not far off.

It was one morning late in the month of April, that Miss Campbell, with her two nieces, were seated at their breakfast, when the postman's knock was heard at the door.

As the servant entered with the letters, the children exclaimed: "Aunt Milicent, I do declare there is one from mamma; do open it at once, and see what it is about."

"Perhaps papa and mamma are coming home," suggested Maud; "or what would be more delightful still, it may be to ask auntie to take us out to India."

"I rather think," interposed Edith, "that the most likely thing is, that mamma has written about our going to school; I shall be sorry if it is."

"When you have quite finished all your suppositions I will read the letter, and very likely you will hear the greater part of it," said Miss Campbell.

"We will keep quite quiet, auntie," replied Edith.

So their aunt read to herself the following, from Mrs. Hamilton.

"My dear Sister,

"I think the time has now arrived when it is advisable for Edith and Maud to go to school, where they will have the advantage of good masters, which at Riversdale is not possible. I am anxious they should be kept strictly to their studies, and believe the discipline of school life will be beneficial, especially for Maud. I cannot tell you how sorry I am to remove them from your watchful care, and the happy home they have had whilst with you.

"In sending Maud amongst so many girls as there are at Madame de Veux, I shall in some respects have cause for anxiety; for, with her natural impetuosity of character, she may be led into doing things which a less impulsive child would shrink from. I have, however, considered the question carefully, and have come to the conclusion, it will on the whole be best that she should go.

"With regard to Edith, if it were not for separating the two sisters, and the desirability for her having 'masters,' for music, etc., I should be inclined to say, education carried on at home would be more suitable.

"You will, I am sure, kindly see that they have all that they may require in the way of clothes, etc.

"I very much regret the school is so far from Riversdale, as it will prevent your seeing them frequently; but I trust that during the long vacations it may be arranged that at least some part of the time they may stay with you. Tell them, with my love, that I shall look forward with anxiety to the accounts Madame de Veux will send me, of their general conduct, and progress in study. I will write to them by the next mail."

Miss Campbell, having told them as much as she thought advisable of the contents of the letter, observed Edith looking very woe begone.

"Oh, Aunt Milicent," she said, "it does seem so miserable to think we have to leave you, when we are so happy. I am sure we would work as hard as we could at our lessons, if we might only remain here. I cannot bear the idea of going to Madame de Veux amongst strangers, and only Maud to speak to."

"They won't be strangers long with us," observed Maud; "and there being such a number will make it all the merrier. So cheer up, Edith; depend upon it after all we shall have some good fun."

Miss Campbell smiled at the little girl's idea of consoling her sister; and rising from the breakfast table, told them to employ themselves in practising at the piano until she should call them.

There was much to be done and thought of in the way of preparation for the departure to school. Miss Campbell had received a letter from Madame de Veux, saying she hoped to see the young ladies after the Easter holidays, which would end in a fortnight.

"Auntie," asked Maud, on hearing this, "are we to have lessons up to the very time? if so, we shall have no holidays at all!"

"No, my dear," replied Miss Campbell; "as you will have to apply yourselves in real earnest to regular and uninterrupted study, when you are at 'La Solitude,' if you and Edith are diligent with your music and drawing you may rest entirely from other lessons."

"Thank you, auntie; now we will try and enjoy ourselves. And, dear me, there's not much time. Come, Edith, away you go to your piano, whilst I try and get on with my drawing, which I must say I am very much interested in. I hope we shall have a good drawing master at school."

The next two weeks passed quickly away. Maud, as usual, full of excitement, allowed her sister to have but little peace; and when expostulated with for being such a torment, reminded her that she must expect plenty of teazing at school, so it was just as well to have a little beforehand, and then it wouldn't come so much amiss.

"I prefer waiting until I am there," replied Edith. "At all events, the thought of all you say we shall have to go through seems to give you great pleasure. I suspect you judge of what our school life is to be from all Harold has told you of his; but I am sure none of the same kind of things would go on at 'La Solitude.'"

"I don't know that!" said Maud, trying to

look wonderfully wise; "it strikes me, setting aside all the tricks, we shall have many a battle to fight; and it's not easy to keep your ground when you are thrown amongst fifty or sixty girls. I can guess pretty well what it will be. However, you needn't believe me; but mark my words, all I say will come to pass."

"I am glad," remarked Edith, "that Helen Murray is going to school at the same time as ourselves: she is always so kind, and ready to help one."

"Helen is all very well," said Maud, "but so dreadfully quiet. Sometimes I have thought there was some fun in her, for she can be merry enough; but as to a trick, I don't believe I should get her to join me in one if I tried for a twelvemonth; she is so awfully stupid in that sort of thing."

"Well, Maud, I don't blame her for not entering into your wild pranks; she shows her wisdom there."

And thus the two children would discuss their future, Maud delighting in conjuring up all the imaginable miseries and trials to which they would be subject.

The eventful morning at length arrived when they were to take their departure from Riversdale, and very sad and tearful they were over their breakfast. One would certainly have thought that Nurse Grey was suffering from a severe cold, so constantly did she make use of her pocket-handkerchief.

Miss Campbell intended accompanying her nieces part of the way, then they would be met by the French governess, who would take charge of them for the rest of the journey.

"Trusty" walked about, his tail and ears hanging down, showing that he knew all was not right.

At last the carriage was at the front door, and the servants carrying out the luggage, but nurse was nowhere to be seen.

"Where can she be?" asked the children.

"Please, miss," said Sarah, "I haven't seen her for the last ten minutes or more, but I think I heard her a crying in the pantry ready to break her heart, only I didn't like to make so bold as to look in."

Maud, on hearing this account, ran off to the pantry, and sure enough there sat poor nurse, the very picture of misery.

"Nurse, nurse, what is the matter?" she asked, throwing her arms round the dear old woman's neck.

"The matter, Miss Maud, the matter indeed! Why, ain't you a going miles away, where I shall never set eyes on you for months together?"

"Oh, don't cry, nurse; very likely we shall come back for the Christmas holidays, so that won't be so long to wait. And here comes Edith; if she sees you upset it will make her in such a state."

Nurse Grey knew that Maud spoke truly when she warned her of Edith's being distressed: so, wiping her eyes, she stood up, and managed to go through the parting scene wonderfully well.

It was a long and somewhat tedious journey they had to take. On reaching the station appointed as the place of meeting with mademoiselle, they alighted, the girls looking anxiously to see what she would be like.

Presently a lady came forward, and introduced herself, saying, "Had she the pleasure of addressing Miss Campbell? She had been sent by Madame de Veux to meet two young ladies."

"You are quite right," replied Miss Campbell; "I hope we have not kept you waiting long." And kissing the children many times, she hurried them into the train, which was on the point of starting.

As the long row of carriages passed by,

Edith's handkerchief was to be seen waving until the train was quite out of sight.

At length their journey came to an end, and getting into a carriage madame had sent to meet them at the station, they reached "La Solitude."

Edith and Maud gave a quick glance at the house, which was a solid red brick building.

Mademoiselle having alighted, desired them to follow her. Crossing a spacious hall, and going down a somewhat long passage, she opened the door of what was evidently a reception room, stiff, both as regarded the furniture and its arrangements.

"I will ask you to wait here, young ladies," she said, "whilst I go and tell madame of our arrival." And she disappeared, shutting the door after her.

The children looked at each other in dismay as they listened to mademoiselle's retreating footsteps.

"How dreadful this is," observed Edith, in a half whisper, "far worse than I expected."

"Yes," replied Maud, "it's rather an unpleasant beginning; but don't be frightened, it may be better than we think. Hush, there's some one coming."

The door was opened by a young girl dressed

in deep mourning, who did not appear to be more than seventeen years of age. Her sweet and gentle expression lighted up with a smile as she spoke to them.

"Will you come with me and take off your things, after which madame will see you for a few minutes before you join the other young ladies."

Much as they dreaded the idea of an interview with Madame de Veux, there was no alternative but to obey.

Following their guide up two flights of stairs, they entered a long dormitory. On either side of the room were ranged the beds. Everything was in such perfect order that it would have been difficult to point out any defect in the arrangements; there was, too, an air of comfort which struck the eye.

Madame de Veux prided herself on her house and its belongings being such that the most critical should not be able to find fault.

By the side of each bed was a small washing-stand, which closed when not in use. A chair for placing the clothes on at night completed the furniture allowed each of the girls. In an adjoining room there was a long row of cupboards, numbered, so that the girls had easy access to their wardrobes when necessary.

Madame's sitting-room, to which they were taken after taking off their jackets and hats, etc., appeared to be some distance from that part of the house occupied by the girls, separated as it was by a long passage.

On knocking at the door, a pleasant voice bade them enter. By a writing table sat a rather elderly lady, whose grey hair was arranged in true Parisian style. Her large dark eyes were full of expression, and her countenance was such as to attract a stranger at once with a feeling of assurance. She welcomed the little girls to what would be for some time to come their home. Observing Edith's timidity and shyness, she addressed herself to Maud, who readily answered any questions asked, feeling wonderfully relieved at finding the much-dreaded interview so different to what she had anticipated.

"You will," said madame, "find your school life strange at first, but after a while will settle down, and, I hope, be as happy as your companions."

Having talked to them for some time, madame rang the bell, and desired the servant to request Miss Danvers to come to her, and when the young governess did appear, consigned the children to her care, telling her to let them join their school-fellows.

Edith had no opportunity of making any remarks to her sister, but managed, by a look of approval, to give her to understand that so far she considered things were going on satisfactorily.

As they approached the schoolroom, the buzz of voices caused them to feel somewhat nervous, for evidently they were about to encounter no small number of girls.

. Miss Danvers threw open the door; immediately every eye seemed to look in that direction, and murmured remarks could be heard on the arrival of the two girls. Miss Danvers was soon surrounded by the young ladies, for she was loved by most of them, and notwithstanding her extreme youth, exercised an influence amongst the greater number which was for their good in every way. She introduced Edith and Maud, and after remaining a short time, left them to attend to other duties.

The schoolroom in which the girls were assembled was large, and fitted up with every convenience. The long benches were at present unoccupied, study being ended, at least for a time.

The young ladies were grouped together in

different parts of the room, some enjoying the fire, whilst others were busying themselves, seated at a table, making fancy articles for a bazaar which was to take place in a short time, whilst some twelve or sixteen of the youngest, whose ages ranged from seven to eleven years, were evidently making the most of the play hour looking over their dolls' wardrobes, a matter of no little interest.

"What a shame," exclaimed a tall dark girl, whose name was Alice Berresford; "I did think Miss Danvers would have remained with us until tea-time; it is so tiresome, we cannot get on without her."

"Yes," replied the girl addressed, "it is very provoking. But, Alice, don't you think we might ask madame to allow her sometimes to give us an hour in the evening, for we shall never get the things finished at the rate we are going on?"

"Oh, no," said Alice, "I should not care to ask. We must manage, I suppose, in the best way we can."

At this moment Miss Danvers re-entered the schoolroom.

"Miss Danvers, Miss Danvers," called several of the girls, "please wait a minute."

Alice Berresford made short work of it by

rushing across the room, and seizing Miss Danvers' hand, declaring she could not possibly leave them before giving advice on one or two matters; "so do come to the table, and see what we are about."

Knowing there was no possibility of escape, Miss Danvers did as she was requested, and no end of things were put before her, cushions to be grounded, the colours of which she must decide upon, screens to be worked, mats, pincushions, and the usual variety of useful and ornamental articles to be seen at bazaars.

Margaret Danvers had a happy way of making things pleasant, and many difficulties were removed before she left them. Whilst giving a few final directions about some braidwork, she felt her dress gently pulled, and on looking round, saw little Gertrude Mansell standing by her side.

"What is it, my dear?" she kindly inquired.

"Please can you spare just one minute?" said the child, pointing to the little ones at the other end of the room. "We have been waiting such a long time; Mabel is in such a state, afraid the tea bell will ring before she has a chance of asking you one word about the new doll's dress."

"Oh, yes, I will come by all means."

And the elder girls good-naturedly allowed their favourite to leave them.

During this time Edith and Maud had been watching with interest all that was going on. The general tone and refined manners of the girls helped to dispel any uncomfortable ideas they had hitherto entertained as to the future.

Maud, turning over in her mind the trials Harold had taken so much trouble to describe, as most surely to come upon them at school, thought to herself, with comfort, " He's quite mistaken, and doesn't understand about girls' schools; I was stupid to believe him. I only hope Edith thinks as I do, or she will be dreadfully timid. I shall try and have a word with her before we go to bed."

Having arrived at this comfortable conclusion, she listened to Miss Danvers, who, with her usual good nature, was entering most thoroughly into the children's interests, advising one thing for the doll's dress, and again some alteration in the hat, which would be a perfect gem when completed.

The important consultation had scarcely come to an end when the tea bell rang.

Perfect silence was observed during meals, for madame was strict in enforcing the rules laid down, punishing any infringement; notwithstanding this, she was much loved and respected by her pupils for her unwearied kindness to each and all.

When the signal was given for the girls to rise, mademoiselle, who sat at the head of the table, announced the pleasing intelligence that they would not return as usual to their studies, as permission was given for recreation during the rest of the evening. "And," continued mademoiselle, "you will be pleased to hear that madame intends paying you a visit in the schoolroom."

The pleasure this news gave was expressed in every face, and they returned to their work in high spirits at the prospect of making considerable progress.

Edith was discovered to be quite competent to help the elder girls; but Maud, attracted by the dolls, was not reluctant to join the merry group of little ones, whose chief employment consisted in making and re-making every article that could possibly be required by dolls of all sizes.

In the midst of their occupations madame entered the room, and after taking a general view of all that was going on, took a seat at the table with the elder girls, interesting herself in looking at each thing as it was handed to her for approval. A happy evening was spent in this way until half-past eight, when, putting away their work, they went to bed.

In a short time the children settled down to the general routine of their school life. Far from regretting having been sent to "La Solitude," they much preferred it to studying at home by themselves. Edith was able to take a very fair stand in the classes, considering her age.

Mrs. Hamilton had been most careful to well ground both the children in the most important part of a child's education, and thus Edith passed an examination in history, grammar, and geography, which would have done credit to one much older than herself.

The two girls were quite familiar with French, as during the past three years they had had a Swiss bonne, whose accent and pronunciation was extremely good. This knowledge was a great help to the children at the present time, as the young ladies at "La Solitude" were expected to converse in French during the day, except at recreation.

Maud was far behind her sister, owing chiefly to her want of application, even allowing for the difference in their ages, which was not more than eighteen months. Whilst, therefore,

Edith was placed in the second class, her sister was put with the younger children. Maud did not appear to consider her position in this respect by any means a painful one. She was able to master without difficulty the lessons given her to learn. The only thing that troubled her was what her Aunt Milicent might think when she should hear of her being so far below Edith.

Helen Murray and Edith became great friends at school, and many a half hour was spent by them in talking of their homes.

From time to time the children heard from Riversdale, Aunt Milicent's letters always being a source of great pleasure to them. She did not fail to give an account of everything she thought might be of interest. But when her letter enclosed one from their mother, it caused no little excitement, and poor Maud was sure on those occasions to fail very signally in her school duties, allowing her thoughts to wander continually from the task before her, (whatever that might be,) to India and all the pleasures she imagined were to be found there.

One morning, when mademoiselle was giving the young ladies the letters which had come for them, she kept one back, remarking,

"And here is one directed to Miss Maud Hamilton."

Maud quickly stepped forward to receive it, her face beaming with joy, for she guessed it was one from her mother. Instead, however, of giving it to her, mademoiselle said:

"No, my dear child, I do not intend you to have it until your studies are finished for the day. Your great inattention at your lessons hitherto, whenever you have had a letter from Mrs. Hamilton, has decided me to detain for the future any that may come for you until the evening."

The change that came over Maud's face on hearing this was certainly very like a dark cloud after sunshine. Greatly disappointed, she left the room, and when alone with some of the younger children, gave vent to a burst of passion, declaring she was determined not to learn a single lesson, even if she was punished severely. Mademoiselle had no right to keep her letters back; it was most unjust and unkind. She hated school, and only wished she was going away that very day. In vain the children tried to soothe her; all they could do or say only seemed to irritate the self-willed little girl.

Edith was not in the room during this

outburst of Maud's temper, having been sent to practice immediately breakfast was over.

How much longer this scene would have continued it is impossible to say, had not the bell warned them to assemble in the schoolroom.

As the girls ranged themselves in their respective classes, Edith observed, on looking at her sister, that something was very much amiss with her, but had no idea what was the cause.

Maud took her place, and sat down with the determination to do wrong, to suffer anything rather than give in.

Each girl had her book before her, and was expected to have her exercise finished and ready for inspection in the course of half an hour. All busied themselves, save Maud, who sat with her hands in her lap.

After a time Miss Danvers, in whose class she was, said, "Maud Hamilton, let me see you pay attention to your lesson."

The child only gave one angry look, and taking her book off the desk, tore as noiselessly as she could the pages, one by one, out of the cover, and crumpling them up, threw them on the ground. Having done this, she certainly felt a little frightened as to the consequences. No one had observed what she had done, except little Gertrude Mansel, who was sitting next to her, and she did not venture to say anything.

When the time came for the girls to take up their books to be examined, Maud went with the rest, but empty handed.

Miss Danvers looked somewhat astonished at seeing her standing without any book, her eyes cast down, and evidently in a very rebellious frame of mind. On asking for an explanation the child remained silent.

"My dear Maud," said Miss Danvers, after waiting in vain for any reply, "where is your exercise book? I cannot allow you to go on in this manner. Tell me, have you written your exercise?"

"No," she answered, "I have not done it, and I don't mean to do it, and I don't care for anything, that I don't. My letter has been kept back, and until it is given to me I won't learn one single lesson."

She said this rapidly and angrily, and then burst into a flood of passionate tears.

Mademoiselle, who was as usual attending to the first class, attracted by Maud's angry voice and crying, immediately sent to inquire the cause of the disturbance, and being informed how matters stood, desired Maud to come to her.

Really frightened, but still unwilling to give in, Maud slowly walked up to mademoiselle, who severely reproved her, and desired her to sit on a form quite apart from every one. "Until," said the governess, "your exercise is correctly written out, and you show by your conduct you are sorry for this act of insubordination, I must insist on your keeping entirely away from the other young ladies."

Maud now felt she had most certainly brought upon herself well-deserved punishment. Even then, if she had only listened to her conscience, which plainly told her how wrong it was to give way to such anger and self-wilfulness, she would not have hesitated to acknowledge her fault, and ask forgiveness. But the little girl's proud spirit rebelled against this, and she resolved to leave the exercise untouched, whatever the consequence might be.

The morning seemed as if it would never come to an end, so tedious were the hours passed by her in stubborn idleness. When at last the young ladies left the schoolroom, and she was alone with mademoiselle, then she knew she would be called upon to give an account of the mis-spent time.

OFF TO SCHOOL. 137

"Maud Hamilton," said the governess, in a severe tone of voice, "bring your slate and come to me."

Maud trembled; she knew she dared not hesitate in doing as she was desired. At that moment she wished, for the first time, she had acted differently. But now she must show the untouched slate, and what would the result be?

When mademoiselle saw no attempt had been made to write the exercise, she was extremely displeased. Leaving Maud standing by the desk, she went to inform madame of what had occurred; then returning, desired Maud to follow her to Madame de Veux's room.

At first Maud was too frightened to look up, for of all persons she feared to vex, it was madame.

"I am indeed shocked to hear of your conduct this morning, Maud," said madame. "I fear you have given way to a rebellious spirit, to a determination to try and get your own way, however wrong that might be. You have defied those in authority, setting a sad example to your school-fellows, especially those who are younger than yourself."

This reproof was said in no angry tone, but as if Maud's disobedience and wilfulness was really a cause of grief to her kind governess.

Madame looked at the little girl standing before her, whose generally bright and merry face was now clouded over with the storm of passion, which was still battling within her. At one moment it seemed as if she would ask for pardon; the next, giving way to the spirit of evil. She ventured, as madame finished speaking, to give one glance, and the sad, kind look she met was enough. Maud no longer listened to any wicked thoughts suggested to her mind, but bursting into tears, acknowledged fully and unreservedly her faults, not excusing herself in any way, but humbly asking to be forgiven.

"Please, please forgive me," said the weeping child. "I am willing to bear any punishment you think I deserve."

Madame took her by the hand, and talked long and earnestly to her of her besetting sin; how surely it would gain a power over her, which, as she grew older, would be the means of much misery to herself and others, unless she now tried, with God's help, to overcome it.

By degrees Maud became calm; already a feeling of relief and thankfulness filled her heart, at having so far triumphed over the evil one.

"And now, my child," said madame, "although you have my forgiveness, it still remains for you to suffer the penalty of your faults. In the first place, you must ask the pardon of mademoiselle and Miss Danvers before all your school-fellows, in whose presence your fault was committed; secondly, the exercise must be correctly written, and during the rest of this week you will forfeit your recreation of an evening. Are you ready to do this, Maud?"

"Yes, madame, quite ready. I shall be glad for every one to know how sorry I am for being so naughty. And please may I do something else as well that will be real pain to me? I wish to do what I shall find very hard to bear."

"What is that, my child?" asked madame, anxious to hear what she had thought of. "If it is anything I think you may suffer for your good, I will give you permission."

"Then please, madame, may I give up having my Indian letter altogether?"

And Maud looked as if this request *did* cost her a struggle, so much did she value a letter from her mother.

"I am glad, my dear child, you have voluntarily asked to do what, I am sure, must be a test of your sorrow; but go now, and remain quietly by yourself, until I send for you this afternoon."

By madame's desire Maud went into a small room close by, only occasionally used for any of the young ladies to see their friends. From the window she could see the girls walking about the garden; amongst them she observed Miss Danvers talking to Edith, evidently speaking of what had taken place that morning. Whilst she stood watching them, she had ample time for reflection, and it was not wasted upon her. She thought of all madame had said, and resolved to try and overcome the one great fault of which she was so often guilty.

In the course of half an hour a servant brought in her dinner. Poor child! she seemed unable to take anything, so full was her heart of anxiety and sorrow.

At half-past two the school bell rang, reminding her, as well as those in the playground, that it was time to apply themselves to study again.

"Now," thought Maud, "I wonder if any one will come for me."

One whole hour passed by, until she began to think she was forgotten. Such, however, was not the case, for presently she heard footsteps; the door opened, and Madame de Veux entered. Maud rose from her seat.

"Are you prepared to come with me?" she asked.

"Yes, madame," replied the little girl.

And following her, they soon reached the schoolroom, where the buzz of many voices repeating lessons could be heard as they entered. In an instant every one stood up. Many eyes fell on Maud, as she stood by madame's side.

Edith turned very pale, and trembled so, that she was desired to sit down, which she did, waiting in painful anxiety for what she might have to hear.

Madame de Veux then addressed the girls, telling them the object of her coming there that afternoon. She felt sure they would rejoice to learn that their schoolfellow, Maud Hamilton, was truly penitent for her insubordination in the schoolroom, and was anxious, in the presence of all assembled, to ask pardon of mademoiselle and Miss Danvers for what she had done.

In a few words Maud did as madame said. Once she nearly broke down, but with an effort succeeded in regaining her composure, and said all she wished them to know.

Having been assured of the pardon asked, she went to the place assigned her, and during the remainder of school time applied herself with diligence to her lessons.

It was a source of great happiness to madame to see how the little girl from this time endeavoured to check the first rising of selfwill that would only too frequently occur. She was not always successful in subduing it, for Maud was young, and she found it difficult to bend her naturally strong will. Often, too, her high spirits and love of mischief made her forget the many resolutions formed of keeping very steady, and then would follow the consequent punishment, either being kept in school during play-time, or, what Maud considered far worse, a reprimand from madame.

We must now pass over some few years, during which time many changes had taken place at "La Solitude." Several of the elder girls had finished their education, and left the school.

Edith Hamilton had made great progress. Her abilities were of no ordinary kind. She was a really talented, clever girl, and loved by all her companions. Madame de Veux had a high opinion of her, and would often remark that she felt all was right in any matter in which Edith was concerned.

It was not without good reason that this was said of her, for she justly merited the esteem of her superiors. Conscientious in all her duties, the young girl had from the very first striven to act on principle; and the effects of her mother's loving care and judicious training showed itself when Edith had to combat with the temptations of school life.

Maud, too, improved in many respects, and although she did not equal her sister in her attainments generally, was on the whole accomplished, and what was still better, well grounded in a solid education.

We must leave them now with Madame de Veux, until they leave their present happy home to join their parents in India. At a future time my young readers may again hear something more of the little girls whose history, I trust, has afforded them both pleasure and instruction.

RICHARDSON AND SON, PRINTERS, DERBY.

PUBLISHED BY

THOMAS RICHARDSON & SON,

23, King Edward Street, City, London;

AND DERBY.

Now Ready, crown 8vo, elegantly bound in superfine cloth, with beautiful design on cover in black, and gold lettering, price 3s. 6d.

CONRAD VALLENROD.

AN HISTORICAL POEM.

BY ADAM MITSKIEVITCH.

Translated from the Polish

BY MICHAEL HENRY DZIEWICKI.

"This Poem holds the highest rank among the creations that enrich Polish poetry. It came from the pen of the very first poet, not only of Poland, but of all Sclavonian countries, and its place among his works is one of the first."—SKETCH BY DR. BELCIKOWSKI.

THERE IS A GOD.

A Reply to

Mr. Bradlaugh's "Plea for Atheism."

BY FRANCIS WINTERTON. Price 4d.

Foolscap 8vo, handsomely bound in cloth, with black printing on side, price 1s.

ELSIE Mc'DERMOTT,

THE LITTLE WATERCRESS GIRL.

BY M. A. PENNELL.

RICHARDSON AND SON'S PUBLICATIONS.

Now Ready, demy 8vo, with Portrait of the Saint, superfine cloth, lettered in gold, price 6s.

THE LIFE OF
ST. JOHN BAPTIST DE ROSSI,
Translated from the Italian,
BY LADY HERBERT.
WITH AN INTRODUCTION ON
ECCLESIASTICAL TRAINING AND THE SACERDOTAL LIFE,
BY THE BISHOP OF SALFORD.

By the same Author,

THE LIFE OF DOM BARTHOLOMEW OF THE MARTYRS, Religious of the Order of St. Dominic, Archbishop of Braga in Portugal, translated from his Biographies. By LADY HERBERT. Demy 8vo, extra cloth, price 12s. 6d.

"Lady Herbert's large Life of this wonderful servant of God—Dom Bartholomew of the Martyrs—has become a standard work on the ecclesiastical spirit, and a perfect treasury for Priests and Bishops."—FROM THE BISHOP OF SALFORD.

Richardson's Popular Catholic Manuals.

Mass for the Dead, Dies Iræ, and Prayers for the Faithful Departed. Price 1d.

Sanctification of Sickness; Practical Instructions for the Comfort of the Sick. Price 1d.

Devotions for the Forty Hours' Adoration, or Quarant' Ore; Solemn Exposition; and Benediction of the B. Sacrament. Compiled by a Priest. 1d.

Marriage, and Family Duties in general. By Archbishop Purcell, of Cincinnati, America. Adapted for English readers by a Priest. Price 1d.

Story of St. Dimas, the "Good Thief." By a Priest. Frontispiece (4th thousand), price 1d.

RICHARDSON AND SON'S PUBLICATIONS.

Now Ready, cloth, red edges, price 6d.

THE HOLY SACRIFICE OF THE MASS.

A DIALOGUE,

In which the Holy Sacrifice, and its Liturgy, Rites, and Ceremonies, are explained.

Fifth Edition, Enlarged, price 1d. in paper wrapper.

THE CHILDREN'S MASS.

With the Approbation of the late RIGHT REV. J. CHADWICK, D.D., Bishop of Hexham and Newcastle.

Second edition, post 8vo, cloth, price 4s. 6d.

LIFE OF VENERABLE JOHN EUDES,

with a Sketch of the HISTORY OF HIS FOUNDATIONS, from A.D. 1601 to 1874. By M. Ch. de Montzey. With a Brief of Approval from His Holiness Pope Pius IX.

SHORT LIFE OF VEN. FATHER EUDES.

From the French. By Father Collins. Demy 18mo, ornamental cloth binding, price 6d.

Second edition, foolscap 8vo, cloth, price 3s. 6d.

LIFE OF ST. ANTHONY OF PADUA,

Friar Minor. Translated from the French.

THE STIGMATA: a History of Various Cases.

Translated from the "Mystik" of Görres. By the Rev. H. Austin. Foolscap 8vo, neat cloth binding, price 3s. 6d.

SILENCE IN LIFE AND FORGIVENESS IN DEATH.

From the Spanish of Fernan Caballero. By the Rev. J. J. Kelly, O.S.F. Foolscap 8vo, handsome cloth binding, price 1s.

RICHARDSON AND SON'S PUBLICATIONS.

NEW SHILLING SERIES OF
CATHOLIC TALES.

Foolscap 8vo, handsomely bound in Cloth, with black printing on side, and lettered in gold.

Elsie Mc'Dermott, the Little Watercress Girl. By M. A. Pennell.

Silence in Life and Forgiveness in Death. From the Spanish of Fernan Caballero. By the Rev. J. J. Kelly, O.S F.

Lassie, and her Guardian Angel. By Charlotte Dean, authoress of "May Templeton."

Eva; or, as the Child, so the Woman. By A. I. O'Neill Daunt.

Queen's Confession; or, the Martyrdom of St. JOHN NEPOMUCENE. By Rev. J. J. Kelly, O.S.F.

Hilda's Victory; & Una's Repentance. By M. F. S.

Little Musicians who became great Masters. First Series. Translated by Mrs. Townsend.

Little Musicians who became Great Masters. Second Series. Translated by Mrs. Townsend.

Ellerton Priory, by the author of "Claire Maitland."

Little Flower Basket. By Canon Schmid.

The Search for Happiness, and other Tales.

Marie, the Fisherman's Daughter.

Godfrey, the Little Hermit. By Canon Schmid.

The Forest Pony, the Gipsy Boy, and other Tales. By Lady Elizabeth Douglas.

The Gift: containing three interesting Tales.

Child-Life and its Lessons. Poetry, Original and Selected.

Elizabeth; or, the Chalet of St. Pierre. By Mrs. Charles Snell.

Isabelle de Verneuil; or, the Convent of St. Mary's. By Mrs. Charles Snell.

To be followed by others.

RICHARDSON AND SON'S PUBLICATIONS.

Just Published.
Demy 18mo, handsomely bound in cloth,
PRICE 6ᵈ EACH.

CATHOLIC TALES
FOR THE YOUNG.

MORNING AND EVENING STAR.	ALTAR FLOWERS.
CHRISTMAS DINNER.	A TALE OF THE CRUSADERS.
HAWTHORN BUSH.	LIFE OF FREDDY WRAGG Br. M. Aloysius, Tertiary O.S.D., by Rev. H. Collins.
PEARL LOST & FOUND.	
THE HOLY HOUSE.	AUGUSTINE MC'NALLY, Tertiary O.S.D., by the Rev. H. Collins.
MAURICE'S TRIAL.	
CARRY'S TRIALS.	WILLIE & HIS SISTERS.

☞ Will be followed by others uniform in size and binding.

SECOND EDITION,
Foolscap 8vo, handsome cloth binding, price 3s.

MIDDLEFORD HALL. A Tale for Children. Edited by the Authoress of "Ellerton Priory," "Claire Maitland," &c.

Francis Willington: or, a Life for the Foreign Missions. By Weston Reay. With a Preface by the Rev. Isaac Moore, S.J. Dedicated by permission to the Bishop of Salford. Crown 8vo, elegantly bound, price 5s.

THE PROBLEM SOLVED. Edited by Lady HERBERT. Crown 8vo, 450 pp., extra cloth, blocked black, with gold lettering, price 6s.

RICHARDSON AND SON'S PUBLICATIONS.

MINIATURE WORKS OF DEVOTIONAL AND PRACTICAL PIETY.

Demy 18mo, handsomely bound in cloth, price 6d. each.

The Snares of the Devil. By John Gerson, Chancellor of Paris. With Biographical Sketch of the Author. *Just Ready.*

Meditations on the Seven Gifts of the Holy GHOST. By Father Pergmayer, S.J.

Communion Prayers for Every Day of the WEEK. By Canon A. C. Arvisenet.

Heavenward. From "Heaven Opened." By Rev. Father Collins.

Month of Jesus Christ. By S. Bonaventure.

Comfort for Mourners. By S. Francis of Sales. From his Letters. Translated by E. M. B.

Stations of the Passion as made in Jerusalem, and Select Devotions on the Passion, from the Prayers of S. Gertrude, O.S.B. Translated by Rev. H. Collins.

Holy Will of God: a Short Rule of Perfection. By Father Benedict Caufield. Translated by Father Collins.

The Our Father: Meditations on the Lord's Prayer. By St. Teresa. Translated by E. M. B.

The Quiet of the Soul. By Father John de Bovilla. To which is added, **Cure for Scruples.** By Dom Schram, O.S.B. Edited by the Rev. H. Collins.

Little Manual of Direction, for Priests, Religious Superiors, Novice-Masters and Mistresses, &c. By Dom Schram, O.S.B. Translated by Father Collins.

Practical Guide to Spiritual Prayer. By John Gerson.

Visits to the Most Holy Sacrament, for every Day in the Month; also Preparation for and Thanksgiving after Communion. By S. Alphonsus Liguori. With an Appendix containing Benediction of the Blessed Sacrament. Cloth, price 6d.

THE LIFE OF S. JOHN OF GOD. By ELEANOR BAILLON. Foolscap 8vo, handsome cloth binding, price 1s.; in paper cover, 8d.

RICHARDSON AND SON'S PUBLICATIONS.

MEDIÆVAL LIBRARY OF MYSTICAL AND ASCETICAL WORKS.

Post 8vo, superfine cloth, lettered.

VOLUMES ALREADY PUBLISHED.

Revelations of Divine Love, shewn to a Devout Anchoress, by name, MOTHER JULIAN OF NORWICH. With Preface by Henry Collins. Price 4s.

Select Revelations of S. Mechtild, Virgin. Taken from the Five Books of her Spiritual Grace, and Translated from the Latin by a Secular Priest. 3s. 6d.

Meditations on the Life and Passion of our LORD JESUS CHRIST. By Dr. John Tauler. Translated from the Latin by a Secular Priest. Price 6s.

The Fiery Soliloquy with God, of the Rev. MASTER GERLAC PETERSEN, throwing light upon the solid ways of the whole Spiritual Life. Translated from the Latin by a Secular Priest. Price 3s.

The Book of the Visions and Instructions of B. ANGELA of FOLIGNO, as taken down from her own Lips by BROTHER ARNOLD of the Friars Minor. Now first translated into English by a Secular Priest of the Third Order of S. Dominic. Price 4s.

Second edition, post 8vo, cloth, price 4s.

SHORT SERMONS, CHIEFLY ON DOCTRINAL SUBJECTS,

Preached in the Chapel of St. Mary's College, Oscott.

BY THE REV. CHARLES MEYNELL, D.D.,

Professor of Theology and Literature at the same College.

The Sermons have this one general aim and character, of TEACHING, rather than exhortation, and may be regarded as exhibiting the results of theological reading, in a popular form, and clear of technicalities.

SHORT MEDITATIONS FOR EVERY DAY IN THE YEAR, according to the Method

of St. Ignatius. Revised by a Jesuit Father. For Pupils in Convent and other Schools.

In Two Volumes, post 12mo, cloth, price 6s. the two vols.
In 12 Monthly Parts, paper wrapper, 4d. each Part.

RICHARDSON AND SON'S PUBLICATIONS.

BERNADETTE — Sister Maria-Bernard. The Sequel to "Our Lady of Lourdes." By HENRI LASSERRE. Translated with the Special Permission of the Author, by MRS. F. RAYMOND-BARKER. Foolscap 8vo, ornamental cloth, price 4s.

Lights and Shadows of Home Affections. A Moral Tale of the Present Epoch. Humbly Dedicated to her virtuous Queen. By the Authoress of "Footsteps through Life;" "Geraldine," &c. Crown 8vo, elegantly bound, 7s.

Father Milleriot, the Ravignan of the Working Men of Paris. From the French of the Rev. Pere Clair, S.J., with the special permission of the Author, by Mrs. F. Raymond-Barker. Foolscap 8vo, cloth, price 2s.

Graziella; or the History of a Broken Heart. An Episode of my Life. By A. De Lamartine. Translated from the French by J. B. S. Foolscap 8vo., cloth elegant, price 2s. 6d.

Heaven Opened; or, our Home in Heaven, and the Way Thither. A Manual of Guidance for Devout Souls. By Rev. Father Collins. Post 8vo, handsomely bound, price 5s.

Legend of the Blessed Virgin Mary, Mother of Christ our Lord. By Michael Henry Dziewicki. In paper wrapper, price 6d.

The Cistercian Fathers, or Lives and Legends of certain Saints and Blessed of the Order of Citeaux, translated by the Rev. HENRY COLLINS. With a Preface by the Rev. W. R. Brownlow, M.A., one of the Editors of "Roma Sotterranea." First Series, 4s.

The Cistercian Fathers. (Second Series.) Translated by Rev. Henry Collins. Price 4s. 6d.

Mediæval Legends, from Cesar of Heisterbach. Translated by Henry Collins. With a Steel Engraving of the Abbey of Mount St. Bernard, Leicestershire. Foolscap 8vo, cloth extra, price 3s.

Farm Boys of Rockstone; or, How are we to know who is Right? Price 2s.

www.ingramcontent.com/pod-product-compliance
Lightning Source LLC
Chambersburg PA
CBHW030315170426
43202CB00009B/1013